كلمة في فقه الدعاء

A STATEMENT REGARDING
FIQH OF DU'AA

SHAYKH 'ABDUR RAZZAAQ BIN ABDIL-MUHSIN AL-BADR

First Edition: Rajab 1434 A.H. / June 2013 C.E.

Cover Design: Strictly Sunnah Designs

E-mail: info@strictlysunnahdesigns.com

Translated by: Aboo Moosaa Raha ibn Donald Batts

Revision of Translation by Rasheed Ibn Estes Barbee

Typesetting and Editing: Aboo Sulaymaan Muhammad
'Abdul-Azim bin Joshua Baker

Subject: Usūl-ul-Deen

Website: www.maktabatulirshad.webs.com

E-mail: Maktabatulirshad@gmail.com

TABLE OF CONTENTS

BRIEF BIOGRAPHY OF THE AUTHOR

<u>His name</u>: Shaykh 'Abdur Razzaaq Bin Abdil-Muhsin Al-Badr.

He is the son of Al-'Allamah Muhaddith of Medina Shaykh 'Abdul-Muhsin Al-'Abbad Al-Badr.

<u>Birth</u>: He was born on the 22nd day of Dhul-Qaddah in the year 1382 AH in az-Zal'fi, Kingdom of Saudia Arabia. He currently resides in Al-Medina Al-Munawwarah.

<u>Current occupation</u>: He is a member of the teaching staff in the Islamic University, in Al-Medina.

<u>Scholastic certifications</u>: Doctorate in 'Aqeedah.

The Shaykh has authored books, researches, as well as numerous explanations in different sciences. Among them:

1. Fiqh of Supplications & Ad-Dhkaar.

2. Hajj & refinement of Souls,

3. Explanation of the book "Exemplary Principles" By Shaykh 'Uthaymeen ﵁ (May Allâh have mercy upon him).

4. Explanation of the book "the principles of Names & Attributes" authored by Shaykh-ul-Islam Ibn Qayyum (May Allâh have mercy upon him).

5. Explanation of the book "Good Words" authored by Shaykh-ul-Islam Ibn Qayyim (May Allâh have mercy upon him).

6. Explanation of the book "Aqeedah Tahaawiyyah".

7. Explanation of the book "Fusuul: Biography of the Messenger ﷺ) By Ibn Katheer (May Allâh have mercy upon him).

8. He has a full explanation of the book "Aadaab-ul-Mufrad" authored by Imam Bukhari (May Allâh have mercy upon him).

From the most distinguished scholars who he has taken knowledge and acquired knowledge from are:

1. His father Al-'Allamah Shaykh 'Abdul-Muhsin Al-Badr—may Allâh preserve him.

2. Al-'Allamah Shaykh Ibn Baaz—may Allâh have mercy upon him.

3. Al-'Allamah Shaykh Muhammad Bin Saleh Al-'Uthaymeen—may Allâh have mercy upon him.

4. Shaykh 'Ali Nasir Faqeehi—may Allâh preserve him.

TRANSLATOR'S FORWARD

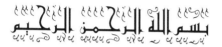

All the praise is for Allaah, the Lord of all that exists. May prayers and peace be upon our Prophet Muhammad, his family, and companions altogether. As to proceed:

Indeed the affair of Du'aa is something which is of the utmost importance within the life of the Muslim; for there is a connection to it within every facet of our lives. From things such as prayer, fasting, and Hajj to things such as using the bathroom, intercourse, and eating, Du'aa is a major part of the life of the Muslim. For this reason, it is a must that one acquires Fiqh in this magnificent act of worship.

Within the hands of the noble reader is the English translation of the small yet beneficial treatise:

كَلِمَةٌ فِي فِقْهِ الدُّعَاءِ

A Statement regarding the Fiqh of Du'aa

This treatise is by the Shaykh 'Abdur-Razzaaq ibn 'Abdul-Muhsin Al-Badr, may Allaah preserve him and his father. The book is concise yet replete with benefit regarding the matter of Du'aa.

As an added benefit, three appendices have been added which are relevant to the subject at hand, also written by Shaykh 'Abdur-Razzaaq, which the reader should find beneficial in aiding him/her to comprehend this matter.

Thanks are due to Maktabatul-Irshaad for the printing and dissemination of beneficial works such as this. Thanks are due to brother Rasheed Barbee for his checking of the translation and sister Umm Yaasir for her typing of the manuscript, and all else who hand a hand in the publication of this work. I ask Allaah to make it a benefit to the Muslims and to place it upon the scales of good for the author, the translator, publisher, and all parties involved in its production. Indeed He is Near and Responsive.

Aboo Moosaa Raha ibn Donald Batts

Durham, NC 11 Rajab 1434/May 20, 2013

INTRODUCTION

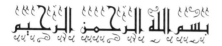

Indeed all the praise is for Allaah; we praise him; we seek His aid; we seek His forgiveness, and we repent to Him. We seek refuge with Allaah from the evil of ourselves and the consequences of our evil deeds. He whom Allaah guides, there is none that can misguide and he whom Allaah allows to stray there is no guidance for him. I testify that none has the right to be worshipped except Allaah Alone, having no partners; and I testify that Muhammad is His slave and Messenger. May Allaah send prayers and peace upon him, his family, and his companions, all together. As to proceed:

Indeed the topic of the Fiqh of Du'aa is a topic which is vast and of the utmost importance; because it is from having comprehension of the religion. It is affirmed within the authentic Hadeeth from the Prophet ﷺ that he said:

مَنْ يُرِدِ اللهُ بِهِ خَيْرًا يُفَقِّهْهُ فِي الـدِّيـنِ .

"He for whom Allaah wants good, He gives him Fiqh (understanding/comprehension) in the religion."[1]

---

[1] Al-Bukhaaree nos. (71, 3116, 7312) and Muslim (no. 1037) from the Hadeeth of Mu'aawiyah, may Allaah be pleased with him.

Therefore, Fiqh of Du'aa is Fiqh in the religion. Rather, it is Fiqh of a great aspect and the utmost importance in the religion of Allaah, the Majestic and High. What indicates this is the statement of Allaah, the Mighty and Majestic:

﴿ فَٱدْعُوا۟ ٱللَّهَ مُخْلِصِينَ لَهُ ٱلدِّينَ ﴾

So, call you (O Muhammad ﷺ and the believers) upon (or invoke) Allaah making (your) religion pure for Him.[2]

Here, He referred to Du'aa as being Deen (i.e. Religion). Likewise, he, the Blessed and High referred to Du'aa as being worship in several verses within the Qur'aan. Allaah, the Mighty and Majestic, has stated:

﴿ وَقَالَ رَبُّكُمُ ٱدْعُونِىٓ أَسْتَجِبْ لَكُمْ ۚ إِنَّ ٱلَّذِينَ يَسْتَكْبِرُونَ عَنْ عِبَادَتِى سَيَدْخُلُونَ جَهَنَّمَ دَاخِرِينَ ﴿٦٠﴾ ﴾

And your Lord said: "Invoke Me, I will respond to your (invocation). Verily! Those who scorn My worship they will surely enter Hell in humiliation! [3]

Here, He referred to Du'aa as worship.

This meaning is affirmed within the Sunnah; within the Hadeeth of An-Nu'maan ibn Basheer from the Prophet ﷺ that he said:

---

[2] (Ghafir 40:14)
[3] (Ghafir 40:60)

الـدُّعَـاءُ هُـوَ الْـعِـبَـادَةُ.

"Ad-Du'aa is worship."4

Rather, It is affirmed within *Al-Mustadrak* by Al-Haakim and others, from the Hadeeth of Ibn 'Abbaas, may Allaah be pleased with him, in a Marfoo' form (that he said):

أَفْضَـلُ الْـعِـبَـادَةِ الـدُّعَـاءُ.

"The best act of worship is Ad-Du'aa."5

Therefore, Fiqh in Du'aa is Fiqh in religion and Fiqh in the worship of Allaah the Majestic and High. So it is a beautiful act of worship and a great act of obedience; it is a magnificent means of nearness which Allaah loves from His slaves.

The research in this subject is very broad, and its aspects are great and extensive. However, I ask Allaah, the Majestic and High, to facilitate for me to bring the pivotal points of this topic and review of some of its significant aspects.

---

4 Sunan At-Tirmidhee (no. 3247) and Al-Musnad 4/267; also Al-Adab Al-Mufrad (no. 714). The 'Allaamah Al-Albaanee, may Allaah have mercy upon him, graded it as Saheeh within Saheeh Al-Adab Al-Mufrad (no. 1757)
5 Al-Mustadrak 1/491. The 'Allaamah, Al-Albaanee, graded it as Hasan within As-Saheehah (no. 1579)

THE VIRTUE OF DU'AA

I will begin, firstly, by clarifying some of the virtues of Du'aa, its status within the Islamic Legislation, and its status within this monotheistic religion; and its status within the Book of Allaah, the Mighty and Majestic, and the Sunnah of his Messenger ﷺ .

He who reviews the Qur'aan will find that the Book of Allaah, the Mighty and Majestic, is replete with many verses and a number of texts indicating the virtue of Du'aa and the loftiness of its status. When you read the Qur'aan, you will find that the first Soorah with which the book of Allaah, the Mighty and Majestic, begins with it; Soorah Al-Faatihah contains this tremendous act of worship, and the last of the Qur'aan Soorah An-Naas as well, contains this tremendous act of worship.

So the Book of Allaah, the Mighty and Majestic, begins with Du'aa and ends with it. The Du'aa, which is within Al-Faatihah, is the greatest of supplications hands down. (It contains) asking Allaah, the Blessed and High, for guidance to the straight path and that the servant avoids the paths of those who are astray and those upon whom is the Anger of Allaah. The last of the Book of Allaah, the Mighty and Majestic, contains the Du'aa of seeking refuge with Him, Glorified and Exalted be He, from the evil of the one who whispers and withdraws; the one who whispers into the hearts of mankind; from the

Jinn as well as men, in order to make them deviate from the straight path of Allaah and the upright way.

Allaah informs us that Shaytaan says:

﴿ ثُمَّ لَأَتِيَنَّهُم مِّنۢ بَيۡنِ أَيۡدِيهِمۡ وَمِنۡ خَلۡفِهِمۡ وَعَنۡ أَيۡمَٰنِهِمۡ وَعَن شَمَآئِلِهِمۡۖ وَلَا تَجِدُ أَكۡثَرَهُمۡ شَٰكِرِينَ ۝ ﴾

Then I will come to them from before them, and behind them, from their right and their left, and You will not find most of them as thankful ones (i.e., they will not be dutiful to You).[6]

So there is no firmness upon the straight path of Allaah, nor safety from the accursed Shaytaan- who calls mankind to deviation from the straight path-except by way of Du'aa and seeking refuge with Allaah, the Majestic and High; and a good manner of taking refuge with Him. This beginning and ending contain an indication of the importance of Du'aa from different perspectives; and the need of mankind for Du'aa to be firm upon the straight path of Allaah. When you reflect upon the other verses of the Qur'aan, you find the great status of Du'aa and lofty station of it within the Qur'aan.

Many verses within the Qur'aan contain the command to make Du'aa and incitement towards it; clarification of its virtue and its

---

[6] (Al-A'raf 7:17)

status and (mention of) that which Allaah, the Blessed and High, has prepared for its people from magnificent reward and abundant bounty and general good within the Dunyaa and the next life. You see, within the Qur'aan, supplications of the Prophets and the righteous from the servants of Allaah and their good connection with Allaah, the Majestic and High. Allaah has said:

$$﴿إِنَّهُمْ كَانُوا يُسَارِعُونَ فِي الْخَيْرَاتِ وَيَدْعُونَنَا رَغَبًا وَرَهَبًا ۖ وَكَانُوا لَنَا خَاشِعِينَ ۝﴾$$

Verily, they used to hasten on to do good deeds, and they used to call on Us with hope and fear, and used to humble themselves before Us.[7]

And Allaah also said:

$$﴿تَتَجَافَىٰ جُنُوبُهُمْ عَنِ الْمَضَاجِعِ يَدْعُونَ رَبَّهُمْ خَوْفًا وَطَمَعًا﴾$$

Their sides forsake their beds, to invoke their Lord in fear and hope.[8]

Likewise, Allaah said:

$$﴿وَاصْبِرْ نَفْسَكَ مَعَ الَّذِينَ يَدْعُونَ رَبَّهُم بِالْغَدَاةِ وَالْعَشِيِّ يُرِيدُونَ وَجْهَهُ﴾$$

And keep yourself (O Muhammad ﷺ) patiently with those who call on their Lord

---

[7] (Al-Anbiya 21:90)
[8] (As-Sajdah 32:16)

**(i.e. your companions who remember their
Lord with glorification, praising in prayers,
etc., And other righteous deeds, etc.)
morning and afternoon seeking His Face. [9]**

Hence, Allaah, the Mighty and Majestic, has
commended the Prophets and the righteous from
amongst His servants for their concern with
Du'aa, and their giving it due importance; and
the excellent manner of taking refuge with
Allaah, the Majestic and High. He informed
within these verses that He responds to them
and that He, Glorified and Exalted be He, will
answer the one who supplicates to Him and give
Him that which he asks for; and he will not
reject a believer who calls upon Him. Allaah
says:

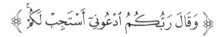

**And your Lord said: "Invoke Me, (and ask Me
for anything) I will respond to your
(invocation). [10]**

And Allaah has said:

﴿ وَإِذَا سَأَلَكَ عِبَادِى عَنِّى فَإِنِّى قَرِيبٌ أُجِيبُ دَعْوَةَ ٱلدَّاعِ إِذَا دَعَانِ ﴾

**And when My slaves ask you (O Muhammad)
concerning Me, then (answer them), I am
indeed near (to them by My Knowledge). I**

---

[9] (Al-Kahf 18:28)
[10] (Ghafir 40:60)

**respond to the invocations of the supplicant
when he calls on Me.[11]**

He also said:

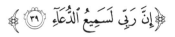

**Verily! My Lord is indeed the All-Hearer of
invocations. [12]**

Allaah informs about Himself, Glorified and
Exalted be He, with that; and that He answers
the supplication of the supplicant and that He is
Near, All-Hearing and Responsive, Glorified and
Exalted be He. All of this is from that which
clarifies to us the status of Du'aa within the
Qur'aan, and that it is a magnificent act of
worship; and it is beloved to Allaah, the Majestic
and High. He, Glorified be He, loves that His
servants supplicate to Him and He loves from
them that they display humility and
humbleness; and that they abundantly seek
salvation from Him and ask Him. He, Glorified
and Exalted be He, loves from them that their
supplications be between them and Him,
secretly and that it be a private counsel.

Allaah, Glorified and Exalted be He, has said:

---

[11] (Al-Baqarah 2:186)
[12] (Ibrahim 14:39)

وَٱدۡعُوا۟ رَبَّكُمۡ تَضَرُّعٗا وَخُفۡيَةً إِنَّهُۥ لَا يُحِبُّ ٱلۡمُعۡتَدِينَ ۝ وَلَا تُفۡسِدُوا۟ فِى ٱلۡأَرۡضِ بَعۡدَ إِصۡلَٰحِهَا وَٱدۡعُوهُ خَوۡفٗا وَطَمَعًا إِنَّ رَحۡمَتَ ٱللَّهِ قَرِيبٞ مِّنَ ٱلۡمُحۡسِنِينَ ۝

Invoke your Lord with humility and in secret. He likes not the aggressors, and do not do mischief on the earth after it has been set in order, and invoke Him with fear and hope; Surely, Allâh's Mercy is (ever) near unto the good doers.[13]

All of this is from that which clarifies to us the status of Du'aa within the book of our Lord, the Mighty and Majestic.

Likewise, when we look into the Sunnah of the noble Prophet ﷺ, and in his brilliant Seerah and his upright guidance, we find the great status of Du'aa and its connection to the life of the Prophet ﷺ; his supplications, his Seerah and his Sunnah, ﷺ. Due to this, there are an abundance of Ahaadeeth from him ﷺ indicating the virtue of Du'aa and the greatness of its status with Allaah, the Majestic and High, and that it is a noble act of worship and a tremendous act of obedience. Allaah loves and is pleased with it for His slaves. From that which has come regarding this is that which is affirmed from our Prophet ﷺ that he said:

---

[13] (Al-A'raf 7:55-56)

مَنْ لَمْ يَسْأَلِ اللهَ يَغْضَبْ عَلَيْهِ

"He who does not ask Allaah, then Allaah is angry at him."[14]

Reflect, may Allaah watch over you, upon this magnificent Hadeeth and its indication of the virtue of Du'aa, its status with Allaah, and the love of Allaah, Glorified be He, for it. He said:

"He who does not ask Allaah, then Allaah is angry at him."

This denotes that Du'aa is beloved to Allaah, and that Allaah, the Mighty and Majestic, loves to hear His servants calling upon Him and beseeching Him privately; seeking from Him and asking Him. And He loves from them that they beseech him by way of that. As the poet said:

اللهُ يَغْضَبُ إِنْ تَرَكْتَ سُؤَالَهُ

وَ بَنِيُّ آدَمَ حِيـنَ يُسْأَلُ يَـغْضَبُ

Allaah is angry if you leave off asking him,

---

[14] Reported in Al-Musnad 2/443,477; also Sunan At-Tirmidhee (no. 3373) and Ibn Maajah (no. 3827) Ibn Katheer said regarding its chain of narration, *"There is no harm within this chain of narration (i.e. the chain is reliable)."* Mentioned within At-Tafseer 4/92. Al-Albaanee graded it Hasan within As-Saheehah (no. 2654) with the wording *"He who does not supplicate to Allaah, then Allaah is angry at him."*

And the children of Adam are angry when they are asked.

The son of Adam gets angry when he is asked, and if this is done frequently to him, then his anger is frequent. As for the Magnificent Lord, the Noble Creator, Glorified and Exalted be He, then He is angry when the servant abandons asking Him. For, the abandonment of asking Him is a form of arrogance. As Allaah, the Exalted has said:

And your Lord said: "Invoke Me, (and ask Me for anything) I will respond to your (invocation). Verily! Those who scorn My worship...

Meaning: he was too proud to supplicate to Me.

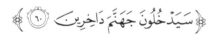

...they will surely enter Hell in humiliation!"[15]

So how can the servant withhold from supplicating to Allaah and be arrogant when he is in need of supplication and asking, to the highest level. He is essentially poor and in need of Allaah, the Glorified and Exalted, from every angle. He cannot do without his Lord for the blinking of an eye; not for one second. He is in need of Allaah, the Mighty and Majestic.

---

[15] (Ghafir 40:60)

As it relates to his food, he is in need of Allaah; as it relates to his drink, he is in need of Allaah; as it relates to his clothing, he is in need of Allaah; as it relates to his guidance to His straight path (he is in need of Him). He is not able to be upright in his religion nor in his Dunyaa, or in the next life except by way of the Tawfeeq of Allah and His favor.

So how can he be arrogant regarding supplication; while he is in need of his Lord, essentially, from every angle. Reflect upon this mater regarding the statement of Allaah, the Glorified and High, within the Hadeeth Qudsee; the Hadeeth of Aboo Dharr which is within Saheeh Muslim.

Allaah, the Majestic and High says:

يَا عِبَادِي ! كُلُّكُمْ ضَالٌّ إِلَّا مَنْ هَدَيْتُهُ فَاسْتَهْدُونِي أَهْدِكُمْ، يَا عِبَادِي ! كُلُّكُمْ جَائِعٌ إِلَّا مَنْ أَطْعَمْتُهُ فَاسْتَطْعِمُونِي أُطْعِمْكُمْ، يَا عِبَادِي ! كُلُّكُمْ عَارٍ إِلَّا مَنْ كَسَوْتُهُ فَاسْتَكْسُونِي أَكْسُكُمْ، يَا عِبَادِي ! إِنَّكُمْ تُخْطِئُونَ بِاللَّيْلِ وَ النَّهَارِ وَ أَنَا أَغْفِرُ الذُّنُوبَ جَمِيعًا فَاسْتَغْفِرُونِي أَغْفِرْ لَكُمْ .

"O my servants, all of you are astray except he whom I have guided. So seek guidance from me and I will guide you. O my servants, all of you are hungry except he whom I have fed, so seek to be fed by Me and I shall feed

**you. O my servants, all of you are naked
except he whom I have clothed, so seek
clothing of me, and I shall clothe you. O my
servants, you commit sins by night and by
day and I forgive all sins so seek my
forgiveness, and I shall forgive you."**

Then He, the Blessed and High, says within this
Hadeeth Qudsee:

يَا عِبَادِي ! لَوْ أَنَّ أَوَّلَكُمْ وَ آخِرَكُمْ وَ إِنْسَكُمْ وَ جِنَّكُمْ
قَامُوا فِي صَعِيدٍ وَاحِدٍ فَسَأَلُونِي فَأَعْطَيْتُ كُلَّ
إِنْسَانٍ مَسْأَلَتَهُ مَا نَقَصَ ذَلِكَ مِمَّا عِنْدِي إِلَّا كَمَا
يَنْقُصُ الْمِخْيَطُ إِذَا أُدْخِلَ الْبَحْرَ

**"O my servants, if the first of you; that last
of you; the human of you the Jinn of you;
were to stand in one elevated space and ask
of me and I were to give every person that
which he requested, that would not decrease
that which is within me anymore than the
needle when it is dipped into the ocean."**[16]

His treasure, Glorified and Exalted be He, is
abundant. The Prophet ﷺ said:

يَمِينُ اللهِ مَلْأَى لَا يَغِيضُهَا نَفَقَةٌ سِحَّاءُ اللَّيْلَ وَ
النَّهَارَ ،

---

[16] Reported by Muslim (no. 2577)

أَرَأَيْتُمْ مَا أَنْفَقَ مُنْذُ خَلَقَ السَّمَاوَاتِ وَ الْأَرْضَ فَإِنَّهُ لَمْ يُنْقِصْ مَا فِي يَمِينِهِ .

"The right Hand of Allaah is full. Spending by night and by day does not deplete it. Have you not seen that which he has spent since the creation of the heavens and the earth? It did not decrease that which is with his right Hand." [17]

Allaah has said:

﴿ مَا عِندَكُمْ يَنفَدُ وَمَا عِندَ اللَّهِ بَاقٍ ﴾

Whatever is with you, will be exhausted, and whatever with Allaah will remain.[18]

For, He gives by way of Speech and He withholds by way of Speech. As He said:

﴿ إِنَّمَا أَمْرُهُ إِذَا أَرَادَ شَيْئًا أَن يَقُولَ لَهُ كُن فَيَكُونُ ٨٢ ﴾

Verily, His Command, when He intends a thing, is only that He says to it, "Be!" and it is![19]

This is His Status, Glorified and Exalted be He. So, how can the servant be arrogant and haughty as it relates to supplicating to his Lord

---

[17] Reported by Al-Bukhaaree (no. 7419) and by Muslim (no. 993)
[18] (An-Nahl 16:96)

[19] (Ya-Sin 36:82)

and fall short regarding Du'aa while he is in need of his Lord, Glorified and Exalted be He, from every perspective? He is in need of his Lord to rectify his food, to rectify his drink, to rectify his clothing, to rectify his dwelling, to rectify his Dunyaa and to rectify his hereafter.

Reflect upon this within the advice of the Prophet ﷺ to 'Aa'ishah, may Allah be pleased with her. The Hadeeth is within Al-Musnad and others. He said:

يَا عَائِشَةُ ! عَلَيْكِ بِالْكَوَامِلِ مِنَ الدُّعَاءِ - وَ فِي رِوَايَةٍ: عَلَيْكِ بِجَوَامِعِ الدُّعَاءِ - : اللَّهُمَّ إِنِّي أَسْأَلُكَ مِنَ الْخَيْرِ كُلِّهِ ، عَاجِلِهِ وَ آجِلِهِ ، مَا عَلِمْتُ مِنْهُ وَ مَا لَمْ أَعْلَمْ ، وَ أَعُوذُ بِكَ مِنَ الشَّرِّ كُلِّهِ ، عَاجِلِهِ وَ آجِلِهِ ، مَا عَلِمْتُ مِنْهُ وَ مَا لَمْ أَعْلَمْ .

"O 'Aa'ishah, upon you is the most complete (form) of Du'aa (in another narration: upon you is the most comprehensive (form) of Du'aa) which is: 'O Allaah, indeed I ask you for all good in this life and the next; that which I know from it and that which I do not know, and I seek refuge with you from all evil in this life and the next; that which I know from it and that which I do not know.'"[20]

---

[20] Reported in Al-Musnad 6/134, 146; also Sunan Ibn Maajah (no. 3846) and Saheeh Ibn Hibbaan (no. 869), also

In another Hadeeth which is within Saheeh Muslim, the Prophet ﷺ said with in his Du'aa:

اللَّهُمَّ أَصْلِحْ لِي دِينِي الَّذِي هُوَ عِصْمَةُ أَمْرِي، وَ أَصْلِحْ لِي دُنْيَايَ الَّتِي فِيهَا مَعَاشِي، وَ أَصْلِحْ لِي آخِرَتِي الَّتِي فِيهَا مَعَادِي، وَاجْعَلِ الْحَيَاةَ زِيَادَةً لِي فِي كُلِّ خَيْرٍ، وَالْمَوْتَ رَاحَةً لِي مِنْ كُلِّ شَرٍّ.

"O Allaah, rectify for me my religion, by way of which my affairs are placed in order. And rectify for me my Dunyaa, in which is my livelihood; and rectify for me my hereafter, to which is my return. Make life an increase for me in good and make death a rest for me from every evil."21

So the servant is in need of Du'aa for the rectification of his religion; the rectification of his Dunyaa, the rectification of his hereafter and the rectification of all of his affairs. The Prophet ﷺ said within another Du'aa:

أَصْلِحْ لِي شَأْنِي كُلَّهُ

"Rectify for me all of my affairs."22

Al-Mustadrak 1/ 521-522. Al-Albaanee graded it Saheeh within As-Saheehah (no.1542)
21 Reported by Muslim (no. 2720)
22 Reported by Aboo Daawud (no. 5090) Al-Albaanee graded it Hasan within Saheeh Al-Jaami' (no. 3377)

So he is in need of asking Allaah; supplicating to Him, and consulting Him in all of his affairs. So how can he be haughty? From that which has come within the Sunnah regarding the virtue of Du'aa is that which has come from him ﷺ that he said:

لَيْسَ شَيْءٌ أَكْرَمَ عِنْدَ اللهِ مِنَ الدُّعَاءِ

"There is nothing nobler with Allaah than Ad-Du'aa."[23]

Sufficient is this as an indication for the status of Du'aa and the greatness of its station and its nobility with Allaah, and that it is a magnificent act of worship and a noble act of obedience. It has a status and a position, and it indicates the love of Allaah for Du'aa and His love for hearing the supplication of the supplicant and consultation of those who consult Him.

From the virtue of Du'aa within the Sunnah, is his ﷺ statement:

أَعْجَزُ النَّاسِ مَنْ عَجَزَ عَنِ الدُّعَاءِ

"The most incapable of the people is he who is incapable of Du'aa'."[24]

---

[23] At-Tirmidhee reported it (no. 3370) as did Ibn Maajah (no. 3829) and Ibn Hibbaan (870) Also Al-Hakim within Al-Mustadrak 1/480. The 'Allaamah Al-Albaanee, may Allaah have mercy upon him, graded it Hasan within Saheeh Al-Adab Al-Mufrad (no. 549)

So the one who is incapable of making Du'aa; then he is of the utmost level of incapability because Du'aa is an act of worship which does not require much effort from the person. It does not make him fatigued nor does it make him sick. He is able to supplicate while he is sitting; and while he is walking and while he is lying down. As Allaah says:

﴿ تَتَجَافَىٰ جُنُوبُهُمْ عَنِ ٱلْمَضَاجِعِ يَدْعُونَ رَبَّهُمْ خَوْفًا وَطَمَعًا ﴾

Their sides forsake their beds to invoke their Lord in fear and hope. [25]

So within every circumstance; one is able to supplicate to Allaah, the Majestic and High. Due to this, the Prophet ﷺ would supplicate to Allaah in all of his situations; when he entered; when exited; when he rode an animal; when he walked; when he rested; when he entered the Masjid and when he exited from it; within his prayer; in all of his circumstances; when he ate; when he drank; when he approached his wife; in all of his situations, he ﷺ would supplicate to Allaah, the Majestic and High. He ﷺ would supplicate to Him in every instance with that which was appropriate for that situation.

---

[24] Al-Bukhaaree reported within Al-Adab Al-Mufrad (no. 1042) as did Ibn Hibbaan within his Saheeh (no. 4498) and At-Tabaraanee within Al-Mu'jam Al-Awsat (no. 5591) The 'Allaamah Al-Albaanee, may Allaah have mercy upon him, graded As-Saheeh the Mawqoof and Marfu' version of this Hadeeth within As-Saheehah (no. 601)
[25] (As-Sajdah 32:16)

Due to that, there are supplications to be said in the morning and the evening; and supplications to be said when going to sleep and when rising from it; supplications to be said within the prayers and when they are completed; supplications to be said when entering and supplications to be said when exiting; and there are supplications to be said when riding. Each supplication which is affirmed from him with his Sunnah is appropriate for the situation in which it is said. This indicates the perfection if his ﷺ guidance, and the beauty and completion if his connection with Allaah, the Majestic and High, in all of his circumstances ﷺ.

It likewise indicates to us the severe need of the Muslim for Du'aa in all of his situations and every circumstance.

The point is that the texts of the book of Allaah, the Mighty and Majestic, and the Sunnah the His Messenger ﷺ which clarify the status of Du'aa and the greatness of its station are very many. I will suffice with that which has passed and move on to the second point.

CLARIFICATION OF WHAT IS DU'AA AND WHAT IS ITS REALITY

The word Du'aa is an Arabic word which is clear in its meaning and evident in that which it indicates. It is a verbal noun for the verb *Da'aa* دعا (He supplicated/invited/invoked) *Yad'oo* يدعو (He is supplicating/inviting/invoking) Du'aa دعاء (supplication/invocation/invitation). It bears the meaning to seek and request. دعاه means: he sought from him and requested of him. Therefore, Du'aa, within the language, means: to seek. How excellent is that with which Du'aa is defined within the legislation; that which Shaykhul-Islaam Ibn Taymiyah, may Allaah have mercy upon him, defined it wherein he said:

$$ هُوَ طَلَبَ مَا يَنْفَعُ الدَّاعِي ، وَ طَلَبَ كَشْفَ مَا يَضُرُّهُ أَوْ دَفَعَهُ. $$

"It is to seek that which will benefit the supplicant and to seek the removal of that which will harm him; or the repelling of it."[26]

Reflect upon this comprehensive definition. Du'aa is to seek and request and to take refuge with Allaah, the Blessed and High. It is either a seeking, which is connected to good; seeking

---

[26] Majmoo' Al-Fataawa 15/10 And see as well Badaa'i Al-Fawaa'id 3/835

after it, desiring it, and diligence upon its acquisition and attainment; or (it is) seeking to repel or remove evil; to defend it before it occurs and to remove it after its occurrence. Due to this, it is affirmed within the authentic Hadeeth that the Prophet ﷺ said:

الدُّعَاءُ يَنْفَعُ مِمَّا نَزَلَ وَ مِمَّا لَمْ يَنْزِلْ

"Du'aa benefits from that which has occurred and from that which has not occurred."27

It removes that which has occurred and it repels that which has not occurred. Hence, Du'aa benefits from both. It is affirmed from him ﷺ that he said:

لَا يَرُدُّ الْقَدَرَ إِلَّا الدُّعَاءُ

"Nothing repels the Qadar except Du'aa."28

From that which is known is that Du'aa is from the Qadar. Allaah, the Glorified and High, decrees for His servant a matter to occur or a matter which is about to occur. So He removes it or repels it by way of his Du'aa. Therefore, Allaah the Glorified and High, has made the Du'aa a reason for the removal of a calamity or

---

27 Al-Haakim reported it 1/670 on the authority of Ibn 'Umar and   Al- Albaanee, may Allaah have mercy upon him, graded it Hasan within Saheeh Al-Jaami' (no. 5721)
28 Reported by Ahmad 5/280 and Ibn Maajah (no. 90). The 'Allaamah Al-Albaanee, may Allaah have mercy upon him, graded it Hasan within As-Saheehah (no. 154)

the repelling of a calamity. Du'aa is requesting Allaah, the Blessed and High, to bring about benefit or to repel harm or to remove harm, due to this. When you reflect upon the general narrated supplications, you find them to be like this. Either requesting Him to bring about benefit, such as His statement:

اللَّهُمَّ آتِنَا فِي الدُّنْيَا حَسَنَةً وَ فِي الْآخِرَةِ حَسَنَةً

"O Allaah, give us good within the Dunyaa as well as within the next life."

Or His statement:

اللَّهُمَّ أَصْلِحْ لِي دِينِي الَّذِي هُوَ عِصْمَةُ أَمْرِي

"O Allaah, rectify for me my religion by way of which my affairs are placed in order."

Or His statement:

اللَّهُمَّ اهْدِنِي فِيمَنْ هَدَيْتَ

"O Allaah, guide me amongst those whom you have guided."

Or his statement:

اللَّهُمَّ إِنِّي أَسْأَلُكَ مِنَ الْخَيْرِ كُلِّهِ

"O Allaah, indeed I ask you for all good."

Or his statement:

رَبَّنَا آتِنَا فِي الدُّنْيَا حَسَنَةً

"Our Lord, give us good within the Dunyaa."

Or his statement:

اللَّهُمَّ آتِ نَفْسِي تَقْوَاهَا

**"O Allaah, give my soul its portion of
Taqwaa."**

These supplications contain asking for the
bringing about of benefit. You ask Allaah, the
Blessed and High, to bring about for you, to
bless you, and facilitate for you that which will
benefit you religiously, worldly, as well as in the
Hereafter. This aspect is from Du'aa which is
connected to bringing about benefit.

The second aspect is connected to that which is
harmful, either the repelling of it before it occurs
or the removal of it after it has occurred. There
are many prophetic supplications wherein we
find this aspect, such as his statement:

وَ قِنَا عَذَابَ النَّارِ

"Protect us from the punishment of the fire."

His statement:

رَبَّنَا اصْرِفْ عَنَّا عَذَابَ جَهَنَّمَ

"O our Lord, remove from us the punishment of the Hellfire."

His statement:

اللَّهُمَّ إِنِّي أَعُوذُ بِرِضَاكَ مِنْ سَخَطِكَ

"O Allaah, indeed I seek refuge with Your Pleasure from Your Displeasure."

His statement:

اللَّهُمَّ إِنِّي أَعُوذُ مِنَ الْعَجْزِ وَ مِنَ الْكَسَلِ

"O Allaah, I seek refuge with you from inability and laziness."

And his statement:

اللَّهُمَّ إِنِّي أَعُوذُ مِنَ الْجُبْنِ وَ مِنَ الْبُخْلِ

"O Allaah, I seek refuge with you from cowardice and stinginess."

And his statement:

اللَّهُمَّ إِنِّي أَعُوذُ مِنَ الْهَمِّ وَ الْحَزَنِ

"O Allaah I seek refuge with you from grief and sadness."

And his statement:

اللَّهُمَّ إِنِّي أَعُوذُ مِنْ قَهْرِ الرِّجَالِ وَ غَلَبَةِ الدَّيْنِ

"O Allaah, indeed I seek refuge with you from being over powered by men and from being overcome with debt."

And his statement:

اللَّـهُـمَّ إِنِّي أَعُـوذُ بِكَ مِنْ مُنْكَـرَاتِ الْأَخْـلَاقِ وَ الْأَهْـوَاءِ وَ الْأَدْوَاءِ

"O Allaah, indeed I seek refuge with you from evil manners, desires, and illness."

The supplications are truly many wherein there is either; seeking the repelling of harm or the removal of harm. When the Prophet ﷺ would come to the sick; he would say:

اللَّـهُـمَّ رَبَّ النَّـاسِ، أَذْهِـبِ الْـبَـأْسَ، وَاشْـفِهِ وَ أَنْـتَ الـشَّـافِي، لَا شِـفَـاءَ إِلَّا شِـفَـاؤُكَ، شِـفَـاءً لَا يُـغَـادِرُ سَـقَـمًا.

"O Allaah, Lord of mankind remove the harm, and heal him, you are the Healer; there is no healing except Your healing; the healing which does not leave any illness."[29]

When 'Uthmaan ibn Aboo Al-'Aas came to him complaining of a pain which he had found within his body, the Prophet ﷺ said to him:

---

[29] Al-Bukhaaree reported it (no.5743) as did Muslim (no.2191) on the authority of 'Aa'ishah, may Allah be pleased with her.

ضَعْ يَدَكَ عَـلَى الَّذِي تَأَلَّمَ مِنْ جَسَدِكَ وَ قُلْ بِـاسْمِ اللهِ

ثَلَاثًا وَ قُلْ سَبْعَ مَرَّاتٍ: أَعُـوذُ بِـاللهِ وَ قُدْرَتِهِ مِنْ شَرِّ مَا

أَجِـدُ وَ أُحَاذِرُ

Place your hand at the place where you feel pain in your body and say Bismillah (in the name of Allah) three times, and say seven times: '(I seek refuge with Allaah and with His Power from the evil that I find and that I fear.'"30

So, you are in dire need of Du'aa in every circumstance and every instance. There is no path to good for you; for you to attain anything of it, except with the help of Allaah and His Tawfeeq; and safety from that which harms and destroys. There is no safety, for you, from evil or any security or protection from anything of it, except by way of the bounty of Allaah and His helping you and protecting you, Glorified and Exalted be He.

This is Du'aa. This is its reality. The reality of Du'aa is asking Allaah and seeking from Him, the Majestic and High, to bring about that which benefits you worldly as well as religiously and in the hereafter; and the repelling of that which harms and removal of it; repelling it before it occurs and removing it after it has occurred.

---

30 Muslim reported it (no. 2202) as did Aboo Daawud (no. 3891) and At- Tirmidhee (no. 2080) and he said: *"It is Hasan Saheeh"* Ibn Maajah also reported (no. 3522)

You, as it relates to all of this, are in need of Allaah, the Glorified and High.

So, reflect here, O successful brother, upon a matter which is of the utmost importance as it relates to Ad-Du'aa, and shows us the clear indication of the great status of Du'aa within the religion.

The beginning point of Du'aa is the heart by way of its need in total poverty before Allaah, the Majestic and High. Due to this, from the means for the acceptance of Du'aa is the presence of heart; that the heart of the individual be present and turn to Allaah, the Majestic and High, as has come within the authentic Hadeeth that the Prophet ﷺ said:

اُدْعُـوا اللهَ وَ أَنْـتُـمْ مُـوقِـنُـونَ بِـالْإِجَـابَـةِ، وَاعْـلَـمُـوا أَنَّ اللهَ لَا
يَـسْـتَـجِـيـبُ دُعَـاءَ قَـلْـبٍ لَاهٍ.

"Supplicate to Allaah while being certain that He will respond and know that Allaah does not respond to an inattentive heart."[31]

Therefore, Du'aa is the presence of heart in the individual and his feeling a sense of need for Allaah and poverty before Him in bringing about benefit for him, religiously, worldly and in all of his situations. So, it is the heart turning to

---

[31] Al-Haakim reported it within Al-Mustadrak 1/493 as did At-Tirmidhee (no. 3479). The 'Allaamah Al-Albaanee, may Allaah have mercy upon him, graded it Hasan within Saheeh Al-Jaami' (no. 245)

Allaah, the Mighty and Majestic, feeling a sense of need; humility for Him; and turning to Him with the tongue in consultation. Due to this, one may know the difference between one who is distressed and other than him. Allaah, the Mighty and Majestic, says:

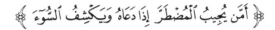

Is not He (better than your gods) Who responds to the distressed one, when he calls Him, and Who removes the evil?![32]

So, the one who is distressed has a fully present heart. His poverty, feeling of dejectedness and humility are for Allaah, the Majestic and High, more so than someone else who is in ease, comfort, bounty, and luxury. You find him such that when he supplicates; perhaps he may move his tongue with Du'aa; however, his heart is not present. Whereas, the distressed one has presence of heart in his consultation, in his asking, and in his distress before Allaah, the Majestic and High; and in his sense of urgency (in need) for Allaah; and he has a good manner of placing his trust in Allaah, the Majestic and High.

As for when the person is in ease, either he will be lax in his Du'aa, and the Du'aa will be minimal, or he will supplicate while his heart is heedless and empty. Few are the slaves of Allaah who, their time of ease, comfort, bounty and

---

[32] (An-Naml 27:62)

affluence is such that he turns to Allaah, the Glorified and Exalted, truthfully in his supplication and consultation. There has come from the Prophet ﷺ, within an affirmed Hadeeth, that he said:

مَنْ سَرَّهُ أَنْ يَسْتَجِيبَ اللهُ لَهُ عِنْدَ الـشَّـدَائِدِ وَالْكُرَبِ

فَلْيُكْثِرْ مِنْ دُعَاءِ الله فِي الرَّخَاءِ

"He whom it pleases him that Allaah should respond to him in times of difficulty and distress, then let him be abundant in supplication to Allaah in times of ease."[33]

The meaning of this is that one turns to Allaah in his time of ease, comfort, contentment, affluence and relaxation. He turns to Allaah and is abundant in supplicating to Allaah and consulting Him, and the sense of urgency and humility before Him; and that his heart is present in the Du'aa and the consulting of Allaah; and not that he simply utters the Du'aa while his heart is heedless.

From the subtleties which we will mention here; is that which Ibn Abid-Dunyaa Has narrated within his book *An-Niyyah Wal-Ikhlaas*.[34] He said:

---

[33] At-Tirmidhee reported it (no. 3382) as did Al-Haakim within Al-Mustadrak 1/544. The 'Allaamah Al-Albaanee, may Allaah have mercy upon him, graded it as Hasan within Saheeh Al-Jaami' (no. 6290).
[34] Hadeeth (no. 5)

"'Umar Ibn Abdul-Azeez passed by a man who had a rock in his hand playing with it while he was saying, 'O Allaah, marry me to one of the Hoor Al-Ayn.' So 'Umar stood and said to him: 'What an evil speaker are you; will you not throw down the stone and be sincere in your Du'aa for Allaah?'"

Meaning: if you want the **Hoor Al-'Ayn**, then strive in your supplication and make it pure for Allaah and do not be heedless, only moving your tongue in Du'aa.

Some of the people raise their hands in their Du'aa and you find him looking to the right, and the left, casting his eyes at that which is moving around him while his heart is heedless as it relates to the supplications. Due to this, it is befitting that one has comprehension of the matter of Du'aa and that the most important of that which is in the affair of Du'aa, is presence of heart and the turning of the heart to Allaah, the Glorified and Exalted, within all of the supplications of the Muslim.

This needs to be paid attention to and one must struggle against his soul to compel it to have presence of heart in order that one may have good thought about Allaah and be abundant and trusting in Him, the Majestic and High, being certain that he will receive a response. Some of the people, as it relates to this matter, when they supplicate they do so in an attentive manner (saying): *Will I be responded to or will I not be responded to.* So one supplicates, for example, saying: *Perhaps it is possible, or maybe.* He does not have certainty. As the Prophet ﷺ said:

ادْعُـو اللهَ وَ أَنْـتُـمْ مُـوقِـنُـونَ بِـالْإِجَـابَـةِ

"Supplicate to Allaah being certain that He will respond."

Therefore, from the important and magnificent aspects of the Fiqh of Du'aa is the presence of heart within the Du'aa of the individual and consulting Allaah; asking and requesting from Allaah, the Majestic and High. For when the heart of the individual is present, and his manner of turning his heart to Allaah, the Majestic and High, is good, the servant beseeches his Lord asks Him, the Majestic and High, from the good of the Dunyaa and the next life.

Here, I will strike some examples for clarity from the narrated supplications. Although I have indicated it in that which has preceded, it is that which is within Saheeh Muslim. The Prophet ﷺ said:

اللَّـهُـمَّ أَصْـلِـحْ لِي دِيـنِي الَّـذِي هُـوَ عِـصْـمَـةُ أَمْـرِي ، وَ أَصْـلِـحْ لِي دُنْـيَـايَ الَّـتِي فِـيهَا مَعَـاشِـي ، وَ أَصْـلِـحْ لِي آخِـرَتِي الَّـتِي فِـيهَا مَعَـادِي ، وَاجْـعَـلِ الْـحَـيَـاةَ زِيَـادَةً لِي فِي كُلِّ خَـيْـرٍ ، وَاجْـعَـلِ الْـمَـوْتَ رَاحَـةً لِي مِـنْ كُلِّ شَـرٍّ .

"O Allaah, rectify for me my religion by way of which my affairs are placed in order, and rectify for me my Dunyaa in which is my livelihood; and rectify for me my hereafter to which is my return and make life an increase for me in good and make death a rest for me from every evil."[35]

When you supplicate to Allaah, the Majestic and High, with the likes of this magnificent supplication, you feel that you are in dire need and that there is an urgent necessity, for the rectification of your religion, your Dunyaa and your Hereafter; and that rectification of that all is within the Hand of Allaah, the Majestic and High. Guidance is within the Hand of Allaah; At-Tawfeeq is within the Hand of Allaah; aid is within the Hand of Allaah; rectification of the Dunyaa, the religion and the hereafter, are all within the Hand of Allaah, the Majestic and High.

Nothing occurs within this universe from movement, nor settlement nor standing or sitting; nor lowering or raising; giving or receiving, except from Him, the Blessed and High, and by His favor, bounty and Tawfeeq. His kingdom, His creation, His servants and the universe are all His possession. He operates therein as He wishes. That which Allaah wills is and that which He has not willed is not. As Allaah says:

---

[35] Its citation has preceded (page 23).

﴿ مَّا يَفْتَحِ ٱللَّهُ لِلنَّاسِ مِن رَّحْمَةٍ فَلَا مُمْسِكَ لَهَا ۖ وَمَا يُمْسِكْ فَلَا مُرْسِلَ لَهُۥ مِنۢ بَعْدِهِۦ ﴾

Whatever of mercy (i.e., of good), Allaah may grant to mankind; none can withhold it, and whatever He may withhold, none can grant it thereafter.[36]

The command is for Allaah, the Glorified and High, from before and thereafter. He gives and He withholds; He lowers and He raises; He gives life; He causes death; He grasps; He strikes; He guides; He misguides. The entire affair is in His Hand. So you believe, with firm creed and complete Eemaan within your heart that the rectification of your Deen, the rectification of your Dunyaa, and the rectification of your Hereafter is within His Hand. Then you take refuge with Him, Glorified and Exalted be He, in a complete and perfect manner; (hoping) that He should rectify these things for you; the religion the Dunyaa and the Hereafter. You begin with the religion, [37] as the Prophet ﷺ began with it.

---

[36] (Fatir 35:2)

[37] We derive from this that the rectification of the religion takes precedence, and that giving due importance to the religion takes precedence. This does not mean that giving importance to the religion means abandonment of giving (primary) importance to the Dunyaa. Due to this, take note of the other supplication, wherein the Prophet ﷺ said:

So rectification of the religion, rectification of the Dunyaa, and rectification of the Hereafter; are all within the Hand of Allaah, the Majestic and High. The Prophet said:

اللَّهُمَّ اجْعَلِ الْحَيَاةَ زِيَادَةً لِي فِي كُلِّ خَيْرٍ، وَاجْعَلِ الْمَوْتَ رَاحَةً لِي مِنْ كُلِّ شَرٍّ.

"O Allaah, make life an increase for me in good and make death a rest for me from every evil."

Reflect upon this affair of the unseen, which is before you. Will your lifespan increase? Will days be decreed for you? Months? Years? Or is it that which remains for you from lifespan is little? What should your affair be in that which is to come and is before you. This is a matter of the unseen. You do not know it. However, you are in need of Allaah, the Glorified and High. And just as you are in need of Allaah, the Glorified and High, to rectify your affairs in your present time; you are in need of Him, the Glorified and High,

---

وَ لَا تَجْعَلِ الدُّنْيَا أَكْبَرَ هَمِّنَا، وَ لَا مَبْلَغَ عِلْمِنَا

"Do not make the Dunyaa the most important thing to us and that which preoccupies our knowledge."

[At-Tirmidhee reported it (no.3502) and graded it Hasan] So there is no harm in giving some importance to the Dunyaa, however the Dunyaa is not to be that which is of greatest importance to you, nor should the Dunyaa be that which preoccupies your mind.

to rectify your affair in that which is to come
from your days.

So, you relegate your affair to Allaah, the
Blessed and High, and take complete refuge with
Him and seek from Him to rectify your religion,
your Dunyaa, and your Hereafter by complete
turning to Him in humiliation before Him and a
good manner of seeking refuge and complete
sense of urgency in seeking (these things from
Him).

This is the reality of Du'aa within the legislation
of Islaam. And know, my successful brother,
that you are in need of Du'aa, which has this
magnificent station within the Islamic
legislation, in everything; within prayer, Hajj,
fasting, Zakat; worldly affairs and in all of your
affairs. You are in need of Du'aa.

And here are some examples of this:

The Prophet ﷺ said to Mu'aadh ibn Jabal:

يَا مُعَاذُ! إِنِّي أُحِبُّكَ ، فَلَا تَدَعَنَّ دُبُرَ كُلِّ صَلَاةٍ أَنْ
تَقُولَ : اللَّهُمَّ أَعِنِّي عَلَى ذِكْرِكَ وَ شُكْرِكَ وَ حُسْنِ
عِبَادَتِكَ

**"O Mu'aadh, indeed I love you. So do not
leave off saying, at the end of every prayer:
'O Allaah, aid me upon your remembrance,**

showing gratitude to you, and excellence in worshipping You.'"38

Reflect here upon this sheer remarkable gesture. Now whenever you pray, and you complete your prayer and at that end of the Salaah, who is the one who has made the prayer obligatory upon you? Who is the one who has made it easy for you to come to it? Was that not Allaah? The companions, may Allaah be pleased with them, would say within their poetry:

وَاللهِ ! لَوْ لَا اللهُ مَا اهْتَدَيْنَا

وَ لَا صُمْنَا وَ لَا صَلَّيْنَا

By Allaah, were it, not for Allaah we would not have been guided,

Nor would we have fasted or prayed.

Where not for Allaah you would not have prayed; and were not for Allaah you would have not fasted; where, not for Allaah you would have not recited the Qur'aan; where not for Allaah you would have not come to the Masjid. So immediately after the completion of your prayer, at its end you should ask Allaah, the Majestic and High:

---

38 Aboo Daawud reported (no. 1522) as did An-Nasaa'ee (no. 1303) Al-Albaanee graded it Saheeh within Saheeh Abee Daawud (no. 1347).

اللَّهُمَّ أَعِنِّي عَلَى ذِكْرِكَ وَ شُكْرِكَ وَ حُسْنِ عِبَادَتِكَ

**"O Allaah, aid me upon your
remembrance, showing gratitude to you, and
excellence in worshipping You."**

You should enter into the upcoming prayer,
and the forth coming act of worship, seeking
from Allaah, the Glorified and High, to aid you
in performing it, and to facilitate for you
the establishment of it. The Prophet ﷺ
said in another Hadeeth, which is connected to
Al-Hajj:

الْحَاجُّ وَ الْعُمَّارُ وَفْدُ اللهِ دَعَاهُمْ فَأَجَابُوهُ، وَ سَأَلُوهُ
فَأَعْطَاهُمْ

**"Those who perform Hajj and 'Umrah are the
delegation of Allaah. He invited them, and
they responded, and they asked Him, so He
gave them."[39]**

Reflect here upon the need of the pilgrim for
Du'aa and aspects of Du'aa within Al-Hajj. The
Talbiyah which is the Du'aa which the pilgrim
repeats many times while coming to Makkah
and in his movements between all of the holy

---

[39] Reported by Ibn Maajah (no. 2893) and Ibn Hibbaan
(no. 4613) also At-Tabaraanee within Al-Mu'jam Al-Kabeer
12/422 on the authority of Ibn 'Umar may Allaah be
pleased with him. The 'Allaamah Al-Albaanee, may Allaah
have mercy upon him, graded it Hasan within As-
Saheehah (no. 1820)

sites, is Du'aa and consulting of Allaah, the Glorified and High.

Reflect upon your asking Allaah, the Blessed and High, for guidance to the straight path which is repeated by you seventeen times a day, by way of obligation and requirement. You say within Surah Al-Faatihah:

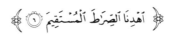

Guide us to the Straight Way.[40]

Shaykh Al-Islaam Ibn Taymiyah, may Allaah have mercy upon him, said:

"Due to this, the most beneficial supplication the greatest of it and the wisest Du'aa is Al-Faatihah, wherein one says:

﴿ اَهْدِنَا اَلصِّرَاطَ اَلْمُسْتَقِيمَ ۞ صِرَاطَ اَلَّذِينَ أَنْعَمْتَ عَلَيْهِمْ غَيْرِ اَلْمَغْضُوبِ عَلَيْهِمْ وَلَا اَلضَّآلِّينَ ۞ ﴾

Guide us to the Straight Way. The Way of those on whom You have bestowed Your Grace, not (the way) of those who earned Your Anger (such as the Jews), nor of those who went astray (such as the Christians).[41]

For when He guides him; , and this is the Siraat. He aids him upon His obedience and

---

[40] (Al-Fatihah 1:6)
[41] (Al-Fatihah 1:6-7)

*abandonment of disobeying Him, so evil will not
afflict him in the Dunyaa nor the Hereafter."*[42]

You ask Allaah, the Majestic and High, to guide
you to the straight path. Were it, not for the
Tawfeeq of Allaah for you, and His aiding you,
you would not be guided to the straight path.
Were it not for the Tawfeeq of Allaah for you and
his aiding you, you would not have been firm
upon this path. Allaah says:

﴿ يُثَبِّتُ ٱللَّهُ ٱلَّذِينَ ءَامَنُواْ بِٱلْقَوْلِ ٱلثَّابِتِ فِى ٱلْحَيَوٰةِ ٱلدُّنْيَا وَفِى

ٱلْأَخِرَةِ ۖ وَيُضِلُّ ٱللَّهُ ٱلظَّٰلِمِينَ ۚ وَيَفْعَلُ ٱللَّهُ مَا يَشَآءُ ﴿٢٧﴾ ﴾

**Allaah will keep firm those who believe, with
the word that stands firm in this world and
the Hereafter. And Allaah will cause to go
astray those who are Zâlimûn (polytheists
and wrong-doers, etc.), and Allaah does what
He wills.**[43]

Also, Allaah, the Majestic and High, says:

﴿ أَفَمَن زُيِّنَ لَهُۥ سُوٓءُ عَمَلِهِۦ فَرَءَاهُ حَسَنًا ۖ فَإِنَّ ٱللَّهَ يُضِلُّ مَن يَشَآءُ وَيَهْدِى مَن

يَشَآءُ ﴾

**Is he, then, to whom the evil of his deeds
made fair seeming so that he considers it as
good (equal to one who is rightly guided)?**

---

[42] Mamjoo' Al-Fataawaa 14/320
[43] (Ibrahim 14:27)

**Verily, Allaah sends astray whom He wills,
and guides whom He wills.[44]**

The Hadeeth Qudsee has already preceded
wherein Allaah said:

يَا عِبَادِي كُلُّكُمْ ضَالٌّ إِلَّا مَنْ هَدَيْتُهُ فَاسْتَهْدُونِي

أَهْدِكُمْ

**"O my servants, all of you are astray except
he whom I have guided. So seek guidance
from me and I will guide you."**

This reality is essential. It is obligatory to
comprehend it within Ad-Du'aa, for it clarifies
for us the reality of Du'aa, and the foundations
of the Fiqh of Du'aa. It also clarifies the fact that
it is a magnificent act of worship and a noble act
of obedience wherein complete humility is
displayed as is complete need and dejectedness
of heart and its turning to Allaah, the Majestic
and High, an excellent manner of consulting
Him in humiliation before Him, the Majestic and
High. Moreover, the Magnificent Lord is
Generous, Excellent, and good. He does not
reject a servant who supplicates to Him nor will
He humiliate a believer who calls upon Him. As
Allaah said:

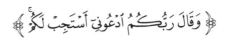

---

[44] (Fatir 35:8)

And your Lord said: "Invoke Me, I will respond to your (invocation)."[45]

He also said:

﴿ وَإِذَا سَأَلَكَ عِبَادِى عَنِّى فَإِنِّى قَرِيبٌ أُجِيبُ دَعْوَةَ ٱلدَّاعِ إِذَا دَعَانِ ﴾

And when My slaves ask you (O Muhammad) concerning Me, then (answer them), I am indeed near (to them by My Knowledge). I respond to the invocations of the supplicant when he calls on Me. [46]

So He, the Majestic and High, responds to the one who supplicates to Him. There has come within the Hadeeth of Salmaan Al-Faarisee from the Prophet ﷺ that he said:

إِنَّ اللهَ حَيِيٌّ كَرِيمٌ يَسْتَحْيِي مِنْ عَبْدِهِ إِذَا رَفَعَ يَدَيْهِ
إِلَيْهِ أَنْ يَرُدَّهُمَا صِفْرًا

"Indeed Allaah is Shy (in a manner that befits His Majesty) and Generous. He is ashamed of His slave, when he raises his hands (in supplication), to turn them away empty."[47]

Meaning: He dislikes allowing his hands to be empty.

---

[45] (Ghafir 40:60)
[46] (Al-Baqarah 2:186)
[47] Reported by Ahmad 5/438 and Aboo Daawud (no. 1488) and At- Tirmidhee (no. 3556) and Ibn Maajah (no. 3865) as well as Ibn Hibbaan (no. 876) Al-Albaanee graded it Saheeh within Saheeh Al Jaami' (no. 2638)

So reflect upon the Generosity; the Goodness; the giving; the favoring; and the bounty. Along with the fact that He is not in need of you or of your Du'aa or of you asking and requesting of Him. However, He loves that from you. From His perfection, Glorified and Exalted be He, and from the perfection of His Goodness and the Perfection of His bounty, is that He, Glorified and High, is Shy from His servant. When the servant raises his hands to Allaah saying: *"O my Lord, O my Lord, O my Lord,"* asking and beseeching Allaah, He is ashamed to turn them away empty handed. Meaning: devoid of having anything in them. All of this is from that which clarifies to us the status of Du'aa it also clarifies to us the reality of Du'aa.

THE GUIDELINES OF DU'AA

From that which is known is that Du'aa has guidelines, conditions and etiquettes. Its status is that of every act of worship. Just as, prayer is not accepted except with its conditions; Hajj is not accepted except with its conditions; fasting is not accepted except with its conditions, and every act of obedience is not accepted except with its conditions, likewise, Du'aa has conditions, guidelines and etiquettes the clarification of which have come within Book of Allaah and the Sunnah of his Prophet ﷺ .

By way of giving them due importance, preserving them, and being mindful of them, that which the individual desires is actualized; which is the answering of the supplication, the settlement of his affairs; the Tawfeeq from Allaah; being aided; firmness; and the rectification of one's ending and the rectification of his Dunyaa. Due to this, it is upon the Muslim, in this regard (i.e., the Fiqh of Du'aa) to comprehend the guidelines of Du'aa and conditions of Du'aa, the clarification of which has come within the Book of Allaah and the Sunnah of His Prophet ﷺ .

From the most comprehensive of verses within the Noble Qur'aan which explain the guidelines of Du'aa and its etiquettes is the statement of Allaah, the Glorified and High, within Surah Al-A'raf:

﴿ ٱدْعُوا۟ رَبَّكُمْ تَضَرُّعًا وَخُفْيَةً ۚ إِنَّهُۥ لَا يُحِبُّ ٱلْمُعْتَدِينَ ﴿٥٥﴾ وَلَا تُفْسِدُوا۟

فِى ٱلْأَرْضِ بَعْدَ إِصْلَٰحِهَا وَٱدْعُوهُ خَوْفًا وَطَمَعًا ۚ إِنَّ رَحْمَتَ ٱللَّهِ قَرِيبٌ مِّنَ

ٱلْمُحْسِنِينَ ﴿٥٦﴾ ﴾

Invoke your Lord with humility and in secret. He likes not the aggressors. And do not do mischief on the earth, after it has been set in order, and invoke Him with fear and hope; Surely, Allaah's Mercy is (ever) near unto the good doers. [48]

Reflect upon the end of this verse wherein Allaah said:

﴿ إِنَّ رَحْمَتَ ٱللَّهِ قَرِيبٌ مِّنَ ٱلْمُحْسِنِينَ ﴿٥٦﴾ ﴾

"Allaah's Mercy is (ever) near unto the good doers"

Meaning: Do good in your Du'aa; do good in your asking; do good in your seeking; give due consideration to the guidelines, conditions and etiquettes of Du'aa; do good in all of this and you shall find the reward for your good doing. You shall find the effect of your goodness you will be given, and you will find bounty, reward and abundant good.

Allaah said:

---

[48] (Al-A'raf 7:55-56)

﴿ إِنَّ رَحْمَتَ ٱللَّهِ قَرِيبٌ مِّنَ ٱلْمُحْسِنِينَ ۝ ﴾

"Allaah's Mercy is (ever) near unto the good doers."

Within the verse attention is drawn to a great deal of etiquettes and conditions of Du'aa. The first and most important of that is at the beginning of the verse within the statement of Allaah:

﴿ ٱدْعُوا۟ رَبَّكُمْ ﴾

"Invoke your Lord…"

Du'aa in itself is worship and should not be given to anyone other than Allaah, nor should one resort therein except to Allaah, the Glorified and High. One should not ask except Allah; nor should help be sought except from Allaah; nor should one seek sustenance, aid, Tawfeeq, uprightness, guidance, and righteousness except from Allah; for all of this is in His Hand, the Mighty and Majestic.

So, none of that should be sought from an angel who is near to Allaah or a Prophet sent as a Messenger or a Walee or other than him. Due to this, the Prophet ﷺ said within his advice to Ibn Abbaas:

إِذَا سَأَلْتَ فَاسْأَلِ اللَّهَ ، وَ إِذَا اسْتَعَنْتَ فَاسْتَعِنْ بِاللهِ ،

وَاعْلَمْ أَنَّ الْأُمَّةَ لَوِ اجْتَمَعَتْ عَلَى أَنْ يَنْفَعُوكَ بِشَيْءٍ ،

لَمْ يَنْفَعُوكَ إِلَّا بِشَيْءٍ قَدْ كَتَبَهُ اللهُ لَكَ ، وَ إِنِ
اجْتَمَعُوا عَلَى أَنْ يَضُرُّوكَ بِشَيْءٍ ، لَمْ يَضُرُّوكَ إِلَّا
بِشَيْءٍ قَدْ كَتَبَهُ اللهُ عَلَيْكَ، رُفِعَتِ الْأَقْلَامُ وَ جَفَّتِ
الصُّحُفُ

"If you ask then ask Allaah if you seek help seek help from Allaah and know that if the Ummah had united to bring about a benefit for you, they would not be able to benefit you with anything except that which Allaah already decreed for you. And if they had gathered for the purpose of harming you, they would not be able to harm you in anything except that which Allaah has already written against you. The pens have been lifted, and the pages have dried."[49]

Therefore, Ad-Du'aa is worship. Allaah, the Majestic and High, has said:

﴿ وَمَآ أُمِرُوٓا۟ إِلَّا لِيَعْبُدُوا۟ ٱللَّهَ مُخْلِصِينَ لَهُ ٱلدِّينَ ﴾

And they were commanded not, but that they should worship Allaah, and worship none but Him Alone. [50]

And Allaah has said:

---

[49] Reported by Ahmad 1/293 and At-Tirmidhee (no. 2516) The 'Allaamah Al-Albaanee, may Allaah have mercy upon him, graded it Saheeh within Saheeh Sunan At-Tirmidhee (no. 2043)
[50] (Al-Bayyinah 98:5)

﴿ أَلَا لِلَّهِ ٱلدِّينُ ٱلْخَالِصُ ﴾

Surely, the religion is for Allaah only. [51]

Due to this, the most pertinent guideline of Du'aa is that it should be purely for Allaah. He who gives this act of worship to other than Allaah, then he is from the most astray of the people. Rather, there is none more astray than him. As Allaah, the Glorified and High, has said:

﴿ وَمَنْ أَضَلُّ مِمَّن يَدْعُواْ مِن دُونِ ٱللَّهِ مَن لَّا يَسْتَجِيبُ لَهُۥ إِلَىٰ يَوْمِ ٱلْقِيَٰمَةِ وَهُمْ عَن دُعَآئِهِمْ غَٰفِلُونَ ٥ وَإِذَا حُشِرَ ٱلنَّاسُ كَانُواْ لَهُمْ أَعْدَآءً وَكَانُواْ بِعِبَادَتِهِمْ كَٰفِرِينَ ٦ ﴾

And who is more astray than one who calls (invokes) besides Allaah, such as will not answer him till the Day of Resurrection, and who are (even) unaware of their calls (invocations) to them? And when mankind are gathered (on the Day of Resurrection), they (false deities) will become enemies for them and will deny their worshipping.[52]

And Allaah, the Majestic and High, has said:

﴿ لَهُۥ دَعْوَةُ ٱلْحَقِّ وَٱلَّذِينَ يَدْعُونَ مِن دُونِهِۦ لَا يَسْتَجِيبُونَ لَهُم بِشَىْءٍ إِلَّا كَبَٰسِطِ كَفَّيْهِ إِلَى ٱلْمَآءِ لِيَبْلُغَ فَاهُ وَمَا هُوَ بِبَٰلِغِهِۦ وَمَا دُعَآءُ ٱلْكَٰفِرِينَ إِلَّا فِى ضَلَٰلٍ ١٤ ﴾

---

51 (Az-Zumar 39:3)
52 (Al-Ahqaf 46:5-6)

For Him (Alone) is the Word of Truth (i.e. none has the right to be worshipped but He). And those whom they invoke, answer them no more than one who stretches forth his hand for water to reach his mouth, but it reaches him not, and the invocation of the disbelievers is nothing but an error.[53]

Allaah, the Majestic and High, has said:

﴿ قُلِ ٱدۡعُواْ ٱلَّذِينَ زَعَمۡتُم مِّن دُونِهِۦ فَلَا يَمۡلِكُونَ كَشۡفَ ٱلضُّرِّ عَنكُمۡ وَلَا تَحۡوِيلًا ۝ ﴾

Say (O Muhammad ﷺ): "Call unto those besides Him whom you pretend [to be gods like angels, 'Eesaa (Jesus), 'Uzayr (Ezra), etc.]. They have neither the power to remove the adversity from you nor even to shift it from you to another person.[54]

None is able to remove it after it has occurred nor is anyone able to divert it before it occurs, defend against it, or remove it except Allaah, the Glorified and High. Allaah, the Glorified and High, has stated:

﴿ قُلِ ٱدۡعُواْ ٱلَّذِينَ زَعَمۡتُم مِّن دُونِ ٱللَّهِ لَا يَمۡلِكُونَ مِثۡقَالَ ذَرَّةٖ فِي ٱلسَّمَٰوَٰتِ وَلَا فِي ٱلۡأَرۡضِ وَمَا لَهُمۡ فِيهِمَا مِن شِرۡكٖ وَمَا لَهُۥ مِنۡهُم مِّن ظَهِيرٖ ۝ ﴾

---

[53] (Ra'd 13:14)
[54] (Al-Isra 17:56)

Say: (O Muhammad ﷺ to those polytheists, pagans, etc.) "Call upon those whom you assert (to be associate gods) besides Allaah, they possess not even the weight of an atom (or a small ant), either in the heavens or on the earth, nor have they any share in either, nor there is for Him any supporter from among them.[55]

Allaah, the Majestic and High, said:

﴿وَٱلَّذِينَ تَدْعُونَ مِن دُونِهِۦ مَا يَمْلِكُونَ مِن قِطْمِيرٍ ۝ إِن تَدْعُوهُمْ لَا يَسْمَعُوا۟ دُعَآءَكُمْ وَلَوْ سَمِعُوا۟ مَا ٱسْتَجَابُوا۟ لَكُمْ وَيَوْمَ ٱلْقِيَٰمَةِ يَكْفُرُونَ بِشِرْكِكُمْ وَلَا يُنَبِّئُكَ مِثْلُ خَبِيرٍ ۝﴾

And those, whom you invoke or call upon instead of Him, own not even a Qitmîr (the thin membrane over the date stone). If you invoke (or call upon) them, they hear not your call, and if (in case) they were to hear, they could not grant it (your request) to you. And on the Day of Resurrection, they will disown your worshipping them. And none can inform you (O Muhammad ﷺ) like Him Who is the All Knower. [56]

Hence, the most important of the conditions of Du'aa and the most important of its guidelines, is to make it pure for Allaah, and that the

---

[55] (Saba' 34:22)

[56] (Fatir 35:13-14)

Muslim never asks except Allaah; nor does he seek aid except with Allaah; nor does he seek sustenance except from Allaah; nor does he present any of his needs and requests and desires for rectification of his worldly affairs, as well as his religious affairs and the affairs of his hereafter except to his Lord and Guardian, in Whose Hands, are all affairs and who controls the heavens and the earth.

Allaah said:

$$﴿ ٱدۡعُواْ رَبَّكُمۡ تَضَرُّعًا ﴾$$

"Invoke your Lord with humility…"

This contains resorting to Allaah and an abundance of asking and perpetually seeking from Him without being hasty. This is from the important affairs as it relates to Du'aa. The Prophet ﷺ stated within the authentic Hadeeth:

$$يُسْتَجَابُ لِأَحَدِكُمْ مَا لَمْ يَعْجَلْ، يَقُـولُ : دَعَوْتُ فَلَمْ يُسْتَجَبْ لِي$$

"The servant will be responded to as long as he does not become hasty and say: 'I supplicated, but I was not responded to.'"[57]

And the Prophet ﷺ also said:

---

[57] Reported by Al-Bukhaaree (no. 6340) and Muslim (no. 2735) on the authority of Aboo Hurayrah, may Allaah be pleased with him.

لَا يَزَالُ يُسْتَجَابُ لِلْعَبْدِ مَا لَمْ يَدْعُ بِإِثْمٍ أَوْ قَطِيعَةِ
رَحِمٍ مَا لَمْ يَسْتَعْجِلْ

**"The servant will continuously be responded
to as long as he does not supplicate for sin
nor the cutting of the ties of the womb and
as long as he is not hasty."**

It was said: *"O Messenger of Allaah, what is
hastiness?"*

The Prophet ﷺ said:

قَالَ : يَقُولُ قَدْ دَعَوْتُ وَ قَدْ دَعَوْتُ، فَلَمْ أَرَ يَسْتَجِيبُ
لِي ، فَيَسْتَحْسِرُ عِنْدَ ذَلِكَ وَ يَدَعُ الدُّعَاءَ

**"That he says, 'I supplicated, and I
supplicated, however, I did not find a
response.' Thus, he becomes frustrated by
that, and he abandons Du'aa."**[58]

Due to this, it is obligatory upon the Muslim to
have humility and abundantly resort to Allaah,
consult Him and ask after asking and seek after
seeking while he trusts that Allaah will respond
to him and bring about that which he hopes for
and give him that which he asks. Allaah said:

﴿وَخُفْيَةً﴾

---

[58] Reported by Muslim (no. 2735) on the authority of Aboo
Hurayrah, may Allaah be pleased with him.

"...and in secret..."

This is a guideline from amongst the important guidelines of Du'aa; that your Du'aa be between you and Allaah, the Glorified and High; that you ask Allaah between you and Him privately consulting Him. Due to this, when the Companions raised their voices with the Takbeer while they were with the Prophet ﷺ on a journey he said to them:

أَيُّهَا النَّاسُ ! ارْبَعُوا عَلَى أَنْفُسِكُمْ، إِنَّكُمْ لَيْسَ
تَدْعُونَ أَصَمَّ وَ لَا غَائِبًا، إِنَّكُمْ تَدْعُونَ سَمِيعًا قَرِيبًا
وَ هُوَ مَعَكُمْ .

"O people, lower your voices, for indeed you are not calling upon one who is deaf nor absent. Indeed you are calling upon one who is All-Hearing, Near; and He is with you (i.e. by His knowledge)"[59]

Therefore, Du'aa is private counsel between the servant and Allaah, the Blessed and High, in secret. In this regard, Al-Hasan Al-Basree, may Allaah be pleased with him, said:

"We have encountered people who there was not upon the face of the earth any action which they were able to do in secret that they would ever do openly. The Muslims would exert efforts in

---

[59] Reported by Al-Bukhaaree (no. 4205) and Muslim (no. 2704) on the authority of Aboo Moosaa Al-Ash'aree, may Allaah be pleased with him.

supplication and one will not hear a sound from them except that of a murmur between them and their Lord, the Mighty and Majestic. This is the meaning of the statement of Allaah, the Exalted:

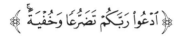

Invoke your Lord with humility and in secret.[60]

And Allaah, the Exalted, mentioned a righteous servant whom He was pleased with within His statement:

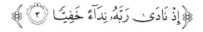

When he called out his Lord (Allaah) a call in secret.[61], [62]

Shaykh Al-Islaam Ibn Taymiyah, may Allaah have mercy upon him, mentioned ten exceedingly great benefits of supplicating in secret. He who desires and seeks to read them will find them within Majmoo' Al-Fataawaa.[63]

Allaah continues:

---

[60] (Al-A'raf 7:55)
[61] (Maryam 19:3)
[62] Reported by Ibn Al-Mubaarak within the book Az-Zuhd (no. 140) Ibn Jareer At-Tabaree transmitted it from him within his Tafseer 10/247-248 and his chain of narration is Hasan.
[63] 15/15-19

$$\text{﴿إِنَّهُ لَا يُحِبُّ ٱلۡمُعۡتَدِينَ ۝ ﴾}$$

"Indeed He likes not the aggressors."

This as well is a guideline from amongst the guidelines of Du'aa which are important; that the Muslim should not be an aggressor in his Du'aa. The greatest of transgression in Du'aa is that one associates a partner with Allaah therein; supplicating to him along with Allaah and asking him. This is the Shirk which expels one from the religion of Al-Islaam.

And from transgression in Du'aa is departure from the Sunnah and the guidance of the Prophet ﷺ by way of falling into innovations and prohibited supplications; also, supplicating for sin and the likes of that from those affairs which oppose the Sunnah; also, falling into that which the Prophet ﷺ has prohibited. Mention has come, within the noble Ahaadeeth of the Prophet ﷺ, of the guidelines, restrictions, and important conditions.

Therefore, departure from his legislation and his guidance ﷺ in this regard is from transgression. The Prophet ﷺ said:

$$\text{إِنَّهُ سَيَكُونُ فِي هَذِهِ الْأُمَّةِ قَوْمٌ يَعْتَدُونَ فِي الطَّهُورِ وَ}$$
$$\text{الدُّعَاءِ.}$$

"There shall be, within this Ummah, people who transgress in purification and Du'aa."⁶⁴

He said this as a warning against that. Due to this, it is obligatory upon the Muslim to beware, lest he should be from those who transgress in his Du'aa.

On the authority of Ibn Sa'd ibn Aboo Waqqaas, may Allaah be pleased with them, who said:

"My father heard me saying: 'O Allaah, indeed I ask you for paradise and its bliss and its delights, and such and such; and I seek refuge with you from the fire its chains, its shackles and such and such.' So he said: 'O my son, indeed I heard Allaah Messenger ﷺ saying:

سَـيَكُـونُ فِي هَـذِهِ الْأُمَّـةِ قَـوْمٌ يَعْـتَـدُونَ فِي الـدُّعَـاءِ

'There shall be a people who transgress in Du'aa'

So beware of being from them. For if you are given paradise then you have been given it and that which is in it from good, and if you have

---

⁶⁴ Reported by Ahmad 4/86-87 also 5/55. Reported as well by Aboo Daawud (no. 96) and Ibn Maajah (no.3864) on the authority of Abdullah ibn Mughaffal, may Allaah be pleased with him. The 'Allaamah, Al-Albaanee, may Allaah have mercy upon him, graded it Saheeh within Saheeh Sunan Abee Daawud (no. 87)

*been saved from the fire, you have been saved from it and that which is within it from evil.'"*⁶⁵

Due to this, from that which he ﷺ would supplicate with the most was the statement:

رَبَّنَا آتِنَا فِي الدُّنْيَا حَسَنَةً، وَ فِي الْآخِرَةِ حَسَنَةً ، وَ قِنَا عَذَابَ النَّارِ

"Our Lord, give us good within the Dunyaa and good within the hereafter and protect us from the punishment of the fire."⁶⁶

Then Allaah, the Blessed and High, went on to say:

﴿ وَلَا تُفْسِدُوا فِي ٱلْأَرْضِ بَعْدَ إِصْلَٰحِهَا وَٱدْعُوهُ خَوْفًا وَطَمَعًا ﴾

"...and do not do mischief in the earth after it has been set in order and invoke Him with fear and hope."

The statement of Allaah:

﴿ وَلَا تُفْسِدُوا فِي ٱلْأَرْضِ بَعْدَ إِصْلَٰحِهَا ﴾

"And do not do mischief in the earth after it has been set in order."

---

⁶⁵ Reported by Ahmad 1/172 as well as Aboo Daawud (no. 1480) . The 'Allaamah, Al-Albaanee, graded it Saheeh within Saheeh Sunan Abee Daawud (no. 1313)
⁶⁶ Reported by Al-Bukhaaree (no. 6389) and Muslim (no. 2690) on the authority of Anas, may Allaah be pleased with him.

Means: after it is been set in order by way of
Eemaan, rectification, Al-Istiqaamah and
worship, at the hands of the Prophets. Do not
corrupt it by way of disobedience and sins. Here,
is an indication that sins, prohibited matters,
and corruption are from the means for the
rejection of Du'aa. Due to this, it has come
within the authentic Hadeeth, the Hadeeth of
Aboo Hurayrah, that the Prophet ﷺ said:

إِنَّ اللهَ طَيِّبٌ لَا يَقْبَلُ إِلَّا طَيِّبًا

**"Indeed Allaah is pure He does not accept
except that which is pure."**

ثُمَّ ذَكَرَ الرَّجُلَ يُطِيلُ السَّفَرَ أَشْعَثَ أَغْبَرَ يَمُدُّ يَدَيْهِ
إِلَى السَّمَاءِ: يَا رَبِّ يَا رَبِّ! وَ مَطْعَمُهُ حَرَامٌ وَ
مَلْبَسُهُ حَرَامٌ وَ مَشْرَبُهُ حَرَامٌ وَ غُذِّي بِالْحَرَامِ، فَأَنَّى
يُسْتَجَابُ لِذَلِكَ؟!

**"Then he mentioned a man who was upon a
long journey being dusty and disheveled, he
raised his hands towards the heavens, and he
said my Lord, my Lord; however, his food is
haram; his clothing is haram; his drink is
haram, and he is nourished upon that which
is haram, so how can he be responded to in
this state?"[67]**

---

[67] Reported by Muslim (no. 1015)

Due to this, one of the people of knowledge said: *"How can you expect a response when you have blocked its path with sins?"*

Therefore, the person is in need of distancing himself from corruption in the earth by way of disobedience and prohibited matters and all types of sins in order that he may be one whose supplication is responded to. Allaah continues:

$$﴿ وَادْعُوهُ خَوْفًا وَطَمَعًا ﴾$$

"...and invoke him with fear and hope."

This is also from the important guidelines of Du'aa that within your Du'aa, you combine Ar-Raghbah (fervent desire) and Ar-Rahbah (fear) and that you be one who is afraid and one who has hope. So, you combine two affairs; fear of Allaah and fear that your Du'aa shall be rejected due to your shortcomings and your weakness and the deficiency in your Eemaan; and that you also have hope and that you have hope and desire for that which is with Allaah, the Glorified and High.

Your state should be like this in your supplication to Allaah and your consulting Him, the Majestic and High. Du'aa has other guidelines and etiquettes, the mention of them would make the speech long. That, which mentioned regarding It, is useful and beneficial if Allaah wills. Al-Badr Ibn Jama'ah poeticized the conditions for the acceptance of Du'aa within his statement: [68]

قَالُـوا شُـرُوطُ الـدُّعَاءِ الْمُسْتَجَابِ لَنَا

عَشَـرٌ بِهَـا بَـشِّـرِ الـدَّاعِي بِإِفْلَاحٍ

طَهَـارَةٌ وَ صَلَاةٌ مَعَهُـمَا نَدَم

وَقْتٌ خَشُـوعٌ وَ حُسْـنُ الـظَّنِّ يَا صَـاحِ

وَ حِلُّ قُوتٍ وَ لَا يُدْعَـا بِمَعْصِيَةٍ

واسْمٌ يُنَاسِبُ مَقْرُونٌ بِإِلْحَاحٍ

They say the conditions for the acceptance of our supplication are;

Ten by way of them the supplicant has glad tidings of success;

Purification, and prayer, also remorse;

The proper time, Khushoo', having a good thought about Allaah, O one who is crying out;

Permissible sustenance and that one does supplicate for disobedience;

---

[68] As is within Al-Futoohaat Rabbaaniyah by Ibn 'Ilaan 7/252.

Using the appropriate name, coupled with a sense of urgency

He gathered ten etiquettes and conditions which are befitting for the Muslim to take into consideration in his Du'aa.

At any rate, as I have indicated within the introduction, the topic of Fiqh Ad-Du'aa is broad. Its aspects are large, and its spheres are numerous. We ask Allaah, the Majestic and High, to give us Tawfeeq to (attain) all good in this life and the next life; that which we know from it and that which we do not know, and to give us refuge from all evil in this life and the next; that which we know from it and that which we do not know, and that He give us Tawfeeq to have goodness in Du'aa and goodness in worship and goodness, in action, and that He guide us to the straight path. Indeed He, the Blessed and High, is All-Hearing, Responsive, and Near.

May prayers and peace be upon our Prophet Muhammad, his family members and companions, all together.

APPENDIX ONE: MISTAKES RELATED TO RAISING THE HANDS [69]

Our speech here is regarding raising the hands in Du'aa. There has preceded speech regarding the benefit of that and its importance in Du'aa and that it is a reason from amongst the reasons of its acceptance due to that which it contains from manifestation of need, submissiveness, and poverty before the Noble Lord. When one stretches forth his hands to Him hoping, asking, displaying humility and Allaah, the Majestic and High, does not return the hands which are raised to Him empty. From that which is obligatory upon the Muslim to pay attention to in this regard, is diligence in knowing the guidance of the Prophet ﷺ in that and following in his footsteps; clinging to his methodology and distance from that which people have invented from descriptions of raising the hands and manners and movements which were not affirmed from the best of the Ummah and the most perfect of them in Du'aa and obedience to Allaah; meaning, Allaah's Messenger ﷺ. It is affirmed within the Hadeeth from the Prophet ﷺ that he said:

---

[69] This appendix was taken from Shaykh 'Abdur-Razzaaq Bin Abdil-Muhsin Al-Badr's book, may Allaah preserve him,: "Fiqh of Supplications and Adhkaar" volume 1 (pages 432-435)

إِذَا سَأَلْتُمُ اللهَ فَاسْأَلُوهُ بِبَطُونِ أَكُفِّكُمْ وَ لَا تَسْأَلُوهُ
بِظُهُورِهَا

**"When you ask Allaah, then ask Him with the
bottoms of your hands and do not ask Him
with the tops of them."[70]**

There has come on the authority of Ibn 'Abbaas,
may Allaah be pleased with him, in a Mawqoof
and Marfoo' form that he said:

الْمَسْأَلَةُ : أَنْ تَرْفَعَ يَدَيْكَ حَذْوَ مَنْكِبَيْكَ أَوْ
نَحْوِهُمَا، وَ الْإِسْتِغْفَارُ : أَنْ تُشِيرَ بِأُصْبَعٍ وَاحِدَةٍ، وَ
الْإِبْتِهَالُ : أَنْ تَمُدَّ يَدَيْكَ جَمِيعًا .

**"Asking is that you raise your hands parallel
to your shoulders or to their level. Al-
Istighfaar (seeking forgiveness) is that you
point with one finger and invocation is that
you extend both of your hands together."[71]**

Shaykh Al-Islaam Ibn Taymiyah, may Allaah
have mercy upon him, said in commenting upon
this Hadeeth:

---

[70] Reported within Sunan Abee Daawud (no. 1486). The
'Allaamah Al-Albaanee, may Allaah have mercy upon him,
graded it Saheeh within As-Saheehah (no. 590)
[71] Sunan Abee Daawud (no. 1489 and 1490) The
'Allaamah Al-Albaanee, may Allaah have mercy upon him,
graded it Saheeh within Saheeh Al-Jaami' (no. 6694)

"For he made them of three levels: pointing with one finger, as is done on the day of Jumu'ah upon the Minbar; the second is: asking; and it is that one raises his hands parallel to his shoulders as is done in most of the Ahaadeeth; the third is that of invocation." [72]

Hence, it is upon the Muslim to look at that which is affirmed from the Prophet ﷺ as it relates to this and cling to it and restricts himself to it, for his guidance is the best of guidance. And the Muslim should beware of that which people have invented and transgressed the limits in this regard.

The Salaf, may Allaah have mercy up them, would beware of placing a narrated description in other than its legislated place, such as the one who raises his hands in Du'aa while he is upon the Minbar on the day of Jumu'ah, and other than the prayer of seeking rain. Although, raising the hands in Du'aa is legislated in other than this place. Muslim reported within his Saheeh on the authority of 'Umarah ibn Ru'aybah that he saw Bishr ibn Marwaan upon the Minbar raising his hands so he said:

قَبَّحَ اللهُ هَاتَيْنِ الْيَدَيْنِ، لَقَدْ رَأَيْتُ رَسُولَ اللهِ - صَلَّى اللهُ عَلَيْهِ وَ سَلَّمَ - مَا يَزِيدُ عَلَى أَنْ يَقُولَ بِيَدِهِ هَكَذَا، وَ أَشَارَ بِإِصْبَعِهِ الْمُسَبِّحَةِ.

---

[72] Refer to the book Ath-Thalathiyaat Al-Musnad by As-Safaareenee 1/653.

**"May Allaah disfigure these two hands.
Indeed I saw Allaah's Messenger** ﷺ **, and
he would not increase upon supplicating with
this hand." And he indicated that with his
index finger."**[73]

So, how about one who innovates as it relates to
the raising of the hands descriptions which have
no basis; or movements which have no
foundations. He who reflects upon the states of
those who supplicate will see from them things
which are startling in this regard.[74]

From that is that some of those who supplicate
raise their hands separately or together to the
level of that which is below the navel or to the
navel. That which is within this, from the
absence of concern and the scanty amount of
importance given to this great matter, is not
hidden.

From them, there are those who, when he
supplicates, separates his hands, the tips of his
fingers are pointed towards the Qiblah, and his
thumbs are pointed towards the sky. It is not
hidden that which is within this from opposition
to the statement of the Prophet ﷺ within
the aforementioned mentioned Hadeeth:

---

[73] Reported within Saheeh Muslim (no. 874)
[74] Refer to *Tas'heeh Ad-Du'aa* by Shaykh Bakr Aboo Zayd
126-129

إِذَا سَأَلْتُمُ اللهَ فَاسْأَلُوهُ بِبَطُونِ أَكُفِّكُمْ وَ لَا تَسْأَلُوهُ
بِظُهُورِهَا

"When you ask Allaah, then ask Him with the bottoms of your hands and do not ask Him with the tops of them."

From them, there are those who turn their hands, when they raise them in Du'aa, in various directions, or they shake them or move them with various movements.

From them, there are those when he supplicates, or before he supplicates, wipes one of his hands with the other or he brushes his hands and the likes.

From them, there are those who kiss his hands after raising them for Du'aa. And this has no basis.

From them, there are those who, when he supplicates, wipes his face with his hands after supplication; this has been narrated in some Ahadeeth; however, it is not affirmed from the Prophet ﷺ. Shaykh Al-Islaam Ibn Taymiyah, may Allaah have mercy upon him, said:

"As for the Prophet raising his hands in Du'aa then, it has come within a number authentic Hadeeth. As for his wiping his face with his hands, then it is not come from him except in one *or two Hadeeths which do not constitute evidence.*"[75]

From the newly invented descriptions as it relates to raising the hands; is kissing the thumbs and placing them upon the eyes upon mention of the name of the Prophet ﷺ with the Adhaan or other than it. A false Hadeeth has been narrated regarding that which is not authentic from the Prophet ﷺ the wording of it is:

"He who says whenever he hears, 'I bear witness that Muhammad is the Messenger of Allaah,' and he says, 'Greetings to my beloved and the coolness of my eyes, Muhammad the son of Abdullah,' then he kisses his thumbs and places them upon his eyes, he will never go blind nor will he ever go bald."

More than one of the people of knowledge has textually mentioned that this Hadeeth is falsehood, and it is not authentic from the Prophet ﷺ.[76]

From the shenanigans of the Soofees is that some of them ascribe that statement to Khidr, upon him be peace.[77]

---

[75] Al-Fataawa 22/519 See also: *Juz' Fee Mash Al-Wajh bil-Yadayn Ba'da Raf'ihimaa lid-Du'aa* by Shaykh Bakr Aboo Zayd.
[76] Refer to *Al-Fawaa'id Al-Majmoo'ah Fil-Ahadeeth Al-Mawdoo'ah* pg. 20
[77] Refer to *Kashf Al-Khafaa'* by Al-'Ajloonee 2/270

From the newly invented affairs as it relates to this is that which some of them do wherein he joins the fingers of his right hand and places them upon his right eye and the fingers of his left hand and places them upon his left eye then he begins to mumble recitation or Du'aa.

From the affairs which are done and are not established from the Prophet ﷺ , is that some of them will place his right hand upon his head after the Salam from the prayer and supplicate. They ascribe that to that which is reported on the authority of Anas ibn Maalik, may Allaah be pleased with him that he said:

"When Allaah's Messenger ﷺ would finish his prayer would wipe his forehead with his right hand and say:

"In the name of Allaah besides Whom none has the right to be worshipped; He is the Most Merciful, the Bestower of Mercy. O Allaah, remove from me grief and sadness."

It is reported by At-Tabaanee within Al-Awsat and Al-Bazzaar. It is a Hadeeth which is not affirmed from the Prophet ﷺ .[78]

From the mistakes in this regard is that some of the worshippers point with two index fingers when saying   At-Tashahhud. It is affirmed within the Hadeeth that the Prophet ﷺ passed by a man who was supplicating pointing

---

[78] Refer to Al-Mu'jam Al-Awsat (no. 2499)

with two index fingers, so the messenger of
Allaah ﷺ said to him:

أَحِّدْ أَحِّدْ

"One, one."

It is reported by At-Tirmidhee. [79]

From those affairs which contradict the Sunnah
in this regard is that some of those who
supplicate specify times wherein to raise their
hands with Du'aa without legislative evidence for
that specification. Such as he who raises his
hands after the establishment of prayer and
before the opening Takbeer; and such as raising
the hands immediately after the Salaam after the
obligatory prayer in congregation, or each time
he prays by himself.

The Noble Shaykh, 'Abdul-'Azeez ibn 'Abdullaah
ibn Baaz, may Allaah have mercy upon him,
said:

*"It is not authentically narrated from the
Prophet ﷺ that he would raise his hands
after the obligatory prayer, nor is it authentically
narrated from his companions, may Allaah be
pleased with them, from that which we know.
That which some of the people do from raising the*

---

[79] Sunan At-Tirmidhee (no. 3557) The 'Allaamah Al-
Albaanee, may Allaah have mercy upon him, graded it
Saheeh within Saheeh Sunan At-Tirmidhee (no. 282)

*hands after the obligatory prayer is an innovation
which has no basis."* [80]

From that, as well, is the raising of the hands in
Du'aa after the prostration of recitation.
Likewise, raising them when seeing the Hilaal
(for the new month), and the likes of that.

In summary, the places which were present
during the time of the Prophet ﷺ, yet it is
not established that the Prophet ﷺ would
raise his hands therein; it is not permissible to
raise one's hands in them because his action is
Sunnah and his abandonment of an action is
Sunnah. And he ﷺ is the excellent example
in that which he brings and that which he
abandons. [81]

That, which is obligatory, is to restrict oneself to
that which has come from him ﷺ and
abandon that which is other than it.

---

[80] *Majmoo' Al-Fataawaa* 11/184
[81] Refer to *Majmoo' Al-Fataawaa* by Shaykh 'Abdul-'Azeez
ibn Baaz, may Allaah have mercy upon him 11/178-183.

APPENDIX TWO: THE SUPPLICANT FACING THE QIBLAH [82]

Indeed from the etiquettes of Du'aa is that the supplicant faces the Qiblah at the time of his supplication. That is because the Qiblah is the virtuous direction which the Muslims have been commanded to face in their acts of worship. So, just as it is a Qiblah for the Muslims in prayer, it is also a Qiblah for them in Du'aa. It has been confirmed that the Prophet ﷺ would face the Qiblah when supplicating within a number of Ahadeeth. From that is that which Al-Bukhaaree and Muslim have reported within their Saheehs from the Hadeeth of 'Abdullaah ibn Mas'ood that he said:

"The Prophet ﷺ faced the Ka'bah and supplicated against a group of the Quraysh, he supplicated against Shaybah ibn Rabee'ah 'Utbah ibn Rabee'ah, Al-Waleed ibn 'Uqbah and Aboo Jahl ibn Hishaam. I bear witness by Allaah that I saw them all killed, and the sun burned them on a hot day." [83]

---

[82] This appendix was taken from Shaykh 'Abdur-Razzaaq Bin Abdil-Muhsin Al-Badr's book, may Allaah preserve him: "Fiqh of Supplications and Adhkaar" volume 1 (pages 436-440)

[83] Saheeh Al-Bukhaaree (no. 3960) and Saheeh Muslim 3/1420)

Muslim reported within his Saheeh from the Hadeeth of 'Umar ibn Al-Khattaab, may Allaah be pleased with him, that he said:

"On the day of Badr the Messenger of Allaah ﷺ *looked at the polytheist while there were a thousand of them, and his companions were three hundred nineteen men. So the Prophet of Allaah* ﷺ *faced the Qiblah then raised his hands and began invoking his Lord saying:*

اللَّهُمَّ أَنْجِزْ لِي مَا وَعَدْتَنِي ، اللَّهُمَّ آتِ مَا
وَعَدْتَنِي ، اللَّهُمَّ إِنْ تُهْلَكْ هَذِهِ الْعِصَابَةُ مِنْ أَهْلِ
الْإِسْلَامِ لَا تُعْبَدُ فِي الْأَرْضِ .

'O Allaah, fulfill that which you have promised me. O Allaah, give that which you have promised me. O Allaah, if this group, from the people of Islaam, are destroyed, then You will not be worshipped in the earth.'

He continued invoking his Lord with his hands raised facing the Qiblah until his cloak fell from his shoulders. So Aboo Bakr came to him, took his cloak, placed it upon his shoulders, and held him from behind and said: 'O Prophet of Allaah, sufficient is that which your Lord has promised you. Indeed He will fulfill for you that which He has promised you.' So Allaah, the Mighty and Majestic revealed:

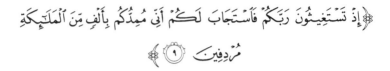

(Remember) when you sought help of your Lord and He answered you (saying): "I will help you with a thousand of the angels each behind the other (following one another) in succession." [84]

So Allaah aided him with angels."[85]

Al-Bukhaaree and Muslim reported on the authority of 'Abdullaah ibn Zayd that he said:

"The Prophet ﷺ went out to his Musllaah to supplicate for rain, so he supplicated and he sought rain then he faced the Qiblah and turned his cloak."[86]

Likewise, facing the Qiblah is affirmed in Du'aa while performing the Hajj upon As-Safaa and Marwah, upon 'Arafah, and upon the sacred sites. Also, at the first and second Jamrah. The Ahadeeth in this regard are many, and they indicate the legislation of facing the Qiblah when making Du'aa and that is the most virtuous and the best thing for the supplicant, although that is not a requirement nor is it obligatory in Du'aa. Because, it is affirmed from the Prophet ﷺ that he supplicated without facing the Qiblah.

---

[84] (Al-Anfal 8:9)
[85] Reported by Saheeh Muslim (no.1763)
[86] Saheeh Al-Bukhaaree (no. 1023, 6343) Also Saheeh Muslim (no. 894)

Imam Al-Bukhaaree formulated a chapter within his Saheeh in the book of supplications titled: **Chapter: Du'aa without Facing the Qiblah.** He reported therein the Hadeeth of Anas ibn Maalik, may Allaah be pleased with him who said:

"Once the Prophet ﷺ delivered the sermon on the day of Jumu'ah when a man stood and said: 'O Messenger of Allaah, supplicate to Allaah to give us rain.' So the sky became cloudy and it rained on us until a man was nearly was not able to make it to his home. It continued raining until the following Friday. So that man or other than him stood and said: 'Supplicate to Allaah to remove the rain from us for we have been flooded.' So the Prophet ﷺ said:

اللَّهُمَّ حَو إِلَيْنَا وَ لَا عَلَيْنَا

'O Allaah, around us and not upon us.'

So the clouds began moving and dispersing around Al-Madeenah, and it did not rain upon the people of Al-Madinah." [87]

It is known that the Khateeb, during the Khutbah, has his back towards the Qiblah. So, this is evidence that facing the Qiblah is not a condition within Du'aa. However, it takes precedence and is better. Shaykhul-Islaam said:

"Due to this, when the Prophet ﷺ would be intense in Du'aa he would face the Qiblah as he

---

[87] Saheeh Al-Bukhaaree(no. 6342)

*did when seeking rain wherein he raised his
hands thoroughly. For it is narrated on the
authority of 'Abbaad Ibn Tameem from his uncle
who said: 'Allaah's Messenger ﷺ went out
to the people and sought rain. So he prayed with
them two Rak'ahs' wherein he recited audibly
and turned his cloak raised his hands and
supplicated and sought rain while facing the
Qiblah.'[88] It is narrated by the group, from the
people of the Saheehs, the Sunan, and the
Masaaneed; such as Al-Bukhaaree, Muslim Aboo
Daawud At-Tirmidhee An-Nasaa'ee, Ibn Maajah,
and other than them. So it informs us that he
faced the Qiblah, which is the Qiblah of the
prayer while supplicating for rain."[89]*

He, may Allaah have mercy upon him, also said:

*"The Muslims are united upon the fact that that
Qiblah which is legislated for the supplicant to
face when making Du'aa is the Qiblah which was
legislated to face during prayer. Likewise, it is
legislated to face it when remembering Allaah,
just as it is faced at 'Arafah and at Muzdalifah;
also, while upon As-Safaa and Marwah.
Likewise, it is recommended for everyone who
remembers Allaah and supplicates to Him that he
faces the Qiblah, as is affirmed from the
Prophet ﷺ that he would intend to face the
Qiblah whenever he supplicated. Likewise, it is
that which is legislated to make the dead face
and, to turn towards the sacrificial animals. So,*

---

[88] Saheeh Al-Bukhaaree (no. 1024)
[89] Refer to *Naqd At-Ta'sees* by Ibn Taymiyah 2/459

*there is not for the Muslims, nor other than them,
two Qiblahs within the acts of worship which are
double-faceted such as prayer and sacrificing, not
to mention acts of worship which are single-
faceted; wherein some of them are connected to
others. For the prayer contains Du'aa within Al-
Faatihah and other than it. And Du'aa, in itself, is
prayer. Allaah has named it prayer within His
Book, when He said:*

$$\text{﴿ وَصَلِّ عَلَيْهِمْ إِنَّ صَلَوٰتَكَ سَكَنٌ لَّهُمْ ﴾}$$

**And pray for them. Verily! Your invocations
are a source of security for them.** [90]

*Also within the Saheeh, there comes, on the
authority of 'Abdullaah Aboo Awfaa that he said:
'The Prophet ﷺ when people would come to
him with their charity would supplicate for them.
My father came to him with some charity so he
said:*

$$\text{اللَّـهُـمَّ صَلِّ عَلَى آلِ أَبِي أَوْفَى}$$

**'O Allaah, send prayers upon the family of
Aboo Awfaa.'** [91]

Allaah, the Exalted has said:

$$\text{﴿ يَـٰٓأَيُّهَا ٱلَّذِينَ ءَامَنُوا۟ صَلُّوا۟ عَلَيْهِ وَسَلِّمُوا۟ تَسْلِيمًا ۝ ﴾}$$

---

[90] (At-Tawbah 9:103)
[91] Saheeh Al-Bukhaaree (no. 1497) And Saheeh Muslim
(no. 1078)

O you who believe! Send your Salât on him (Muhammad ﷺ), and greet him with the Islâmic way of greeting.[92]

The Prophet ﷺ taught his Ummah how to send the prayers upon him in many Ahadeeth within the Saheeh books and other than them, and in all of them he taught them to supplicate for him; that Allaah sends prayers and blessings upon him."[93]

He mentioned that in the context of his refutation against those who reject the Highness of Allaah, such as the Jahmiyah and those who are affected by them from the people of desires, when they claimed that raising the hands up when supplicating is only legislated because the heavens is the Qiblah of Du'aa just as the Ka'bah is the Qiblah of prayer. So they, by way of that, have made two Qiblahs for the Muslims; a Qiblah for supplication which is the sky and a Qiblah for prayer which is the Ka'bah. What has resorted them to this is a corrupt affirmation and their rejection of the Loftiness of the Lord, the Blessed and High, above His creation, and their arbitrariness in interpreting many texts, which indicate the Highness of Allaah, in other than their apparent and intended meanings, by way of various distortions and various deviations which, in reality, are a deviation regarding the verses of Allaah, His Names and His Attributes. Allaah says:

---

[92] (Al-Ahzab 33:56)
[93] Refer to Naqd At-Ta'sees 2/452-453.

﴿ وَذَرُوا۟ ٱلَّذِينَ يُلْحِدُونَ فِىٓ أَسْمَٰٓئِهِۦٓ ۚ سَيُجْزَوْنَ مَا كَانُوا۟ يَعْمَلُونَ ۝ ﴾

**And leave the company of those who belie or
deny (or utter impious speech against) His
Names. They will be requited for what they
used to do.**[94]

And Allaah also says:

﴿ إِنَّ ٱلَّذِينَ يُلْحِدُونَ فِىٓ ءَايَٰتِنَا لَا يَخْفَوْنَ عَلَيْنَآ ﴾

**Verily, those who turn away from Our Ayât
are not hidden from Us.**[95]

And the Shaykh, may Allaah have mercy upon
him, clarified, in the context of his refutation
against them, that the Qiblah is that which the
person faces and facing is the opposite of one
turning his back. Therefore, the Qiblah is that
which the individual faces and not that which he
turns his back towards. As for that towards
which the individual raises his hands or his
head or his vision, then this, by way of
agreement of the people (of knowledge) is not
referred to as Qiblah, because the person does
not face it just as he does not turn his back
towards the direction to which he faces. He who
faces something then he has turned his back to
that which opposes it. Just as he who faces the
Ka'bah has turned his back to that which is
opposition to the Ka'bah. It is known that the

---

[94] (Al-A'raf 7:180)
[95] (Fussilat 41:40)

supplicant is not facing the heavens nor is his back towards the earth. Rather, he is facing some directions, either the Qiblah or other than it; and his back is towards that which opposes it, such as the one making prayer. So, it is clear that considering that to be the Qiblah is false by way of the intellect, the language, and the legislation. It is clear and evident falsehood to everyone. [96]

That, which is intended, is that the Qiblah of the Muslims in Du'aa is their Qiblah within prayer. As for their raising their hands, when supplicating, towards the heavens, this is because their Lord, to Whom they are supplicating, asking, hoping, and desiring to attain His reward and mercy and whom they fear, is above His heavens over His throne; High Exalted above His creation. He hears their supplications and He responds to their invocations just He has said:

$$﴿ٱلرَّحْمَٰنُ عَلَى ٱلْعَرْشِ ٱسْتَوَىٰ ۝ لَهُۥ مَا فِى ٱلسَّمَٰوَٰتِ وَمَا فِى ٱلْأَرْضِ وَمَا بَيْنَهُمَا وَمَا تَحْتَ ٱلثَّرَىٰ ۝ وَإِن تَجْهَرْ بِٱلْقَوْلِ فَإِنَّهُۥ يَعْلَمُ ٱلسِّرَّ وَأَخْفَى ۝ ٱللَّهُ لَآ إِلَٰهَ إِلَّا هُوَ لَهُ ٱلْأَسْمَآءُ ٱلْحُسْنَىٰ ۝ ﴾$$

The Most Beneficent (Allaah) Istawa (rose over) the (Mighty) Throne (in a manner that suits His Majesty). To Him belong all that is in the heavens and all that is on the earth, and all that is between them, and all that is

---

[96] Refer to Naqd At-Ta'sees 2/462.

under the soil. And if you (O
Muhammad ﷺ) speak (the invocation)
aloud, then verily, He knows the secret and
that which is yet more hidden. Allaah! Laa
Ilaha Illa Huwa (none has the right to be
worshipped but He)! To Him belong the Best
Names.[97]

---

[97] (Ta-Ha 20:5-8)

APPENDIX THREE: FROM THE ETIQUETTES OF DU'AA [98]

Indeed from the important guidelines of Du'aa and its magnificent etiquettes is that the Muslim begins his Du'aa by praising his Lord with that which He is deserving of from Noble Qualities and Attributes of Greatness and Perfection and that he mentions His Greatness, His Bounty, His Generosity, and the Magnificence of His Favor. That is the most comprehensive of that which the one asking and requesting can do; praise his Lord, laud Him, Glorify Him, and mention His favors and blessings. All of that should be placed at the beginning of his request as a means for the acceptance and that about which will bring a response. He who reflects up the supplications which have come in the Book and the Sunnah will find that many of them begin with praising Allaah, mentioning His favors and blessings, and acknowledging His bounty, generosity, and blessings.

From the likes of that is the great Du'aa which is contained within Surah Al-Faatihah; which is the greatest of the chapters of the Noble Qur'aan and the most noble of them, due to it comprising the most excellent manner of requesting and the highest of noble objectives. Shaykh Al –Islaam

---

[98] This appendix was taken from Shaykh 'Abdur-Razzaaq Bin Abdil-Muhsin Al-Badr's book, may Allaah preserve him: "Fiqh of Supplications and Adhkaar" volume 1 (pages 441-444)

Ibn Taymiyah, may Allaah have mercy upon him, said:

"Due to this, the most beneficial supplication, the greatest of them, and the wisest is the Du'aa of Al-Faatihah, wherein one says:

Guide us to the Straight Way. The Way of those on whom You have bestowed Your Grace, not (the way) of those who earned Your Anger (such as the Jews), nor of those who went astray (such as the Christians).[99]

For if He guides him to the straight path then He aids him upon obedience to Him and leaving off disobedience to Him. So evil will not afflict him in the Dunyaa not the Hereafter."[100]

So, this magnificent Du'aa begins with praising Allaah, lauding Him, and glorifying Him; (which is) from that which is a reason for its acceptance and a key to the answering of one's supplication. That which clarifies and makes it evident is that which has come within Saheeh Muslim from the Hadeeth of Aboo Hurayrah, may Allaah be pleased with him, who said:

"I heard Allaah's Messenger ﷺ saying:

---

[99] (Al-Fatihah 1:6-7)
[100] Majmoo' Al-Fataawaa 8/215-216

قَالَ اللهُ : قَسَمْتُ الصَّلَاةَ بَيْنِي وَ بَيْنَ عَبْدِي نِصْفَيْنِ ،

وَ لِعَبْدِي مَا سَأَلَ ، فَإِذَا قَالَ الْعَبْدُ : ﴿ٱلْحَمْدُ لِلَّهِ رَبِّ

ٱلْعَٰلَمِينَ ﴾ قَالَ اللهُ تَعَالَى : حَمِدَنِي عَبْدِي ، وَ إِذَا قَالَ

﴿ٱلرَّحْمَٰنِ ٱلرَّحِيمِ ﴾ قَالَ اللهُ تَعَالَى : أَثْنَى عَلَيَّ عَبْدِي ، وَ إِذَا

قَالَ ﴿مَٰلِكِ يَوْمِ ٱلدِّينِ ﴾ قَالَ اللهُ تَعَالَى : مَجَّدَنِي عَبْدِي ، وَ

قَالَ مَرَّةً : فَوَّضَ إِلَيَّ عَبْدِي ، فَإِذَا قَالَ ﴿إِيَّاكَ نَعْبُدُ وَإِيَّاكَ

نَسْتَعِينُ ﴾ قَالَ : هَذِهِ بَيْنِي وَ بَيْنَ عَبْدِي ، وَلِعَبْدِي مَا

سَأَلَ ، فَإِذَا قَالَ ﴿ٱهْدِنَا ٱلصِّرَٰطَ ٱلْمُسْتَقِيمَ ۝ صِرَٰطَ ٱلَّذِينَ أَنْعَمْتَ عَلَيْهِمْ غَيْرِ

ٱلْمَغْضُوبِ عَلَيْهِمْ وَلَا ٱلضَّآلِّينَ ﴾ قَالَ هَذَا لِعَبْدِي وَ لِعَبْدِي مَا

سَأَلَ

**'Allaah has said I have divided the prayer
between Me and my servant into two halves
and for my servant is that which he has
asked for so when the servant says: 'All the
praise is for Allaah, the Lord of all that
exists,' Allaah says: 'My servant has praised
Me. And when the servant says: 'The Most
Merciful, the Bestower of Mercy,' Allaah says:
'My servant has lauded Me.' And when He
says: 'Master of the Day of Recompense,'
Allaah, the Exalted, says: 'My servant has
Glorified Me,' And then he says My servant
has entrusted his affairs to me.' So, when he**

says: 'You Alone we worship and You Alone we ask for help.' Allaah says 'This is between Me and My servant and My servant shall have that which he asked for.' And when he says: 'Guide us to the straight path. The path of those upon whom is your favor; not the path of those who have earned Your anger nor of those who have gone astray.' Allaah says: 'This is for my servant and my servant shall have that which he asked for.'"[101]

So, Allaah, the Glorified, has taught His servants, within this magnificent Soorah, how to supplicate to Him, ask Him and seek nearness to Him. Ibnul-Qayyim may Allaah have mercy upon him said:

"Since asking Allaah for guidance to the straight path is the most noble of requests and attainment of it is the most dignified bounty, Allaah taught his servants how to ask Him and He commanded them to begin it with praising Him, lauding Him, and Glorifying Him; then He mentioned their worship and their Tawheed. So, these two are means to that which they request; seeking nearness to Him by way of His Names and His Attributes and seeking nearness to Him by way of His worship. These two means of nearness, nearly no Du'aa is rejected along with them..."

Up until he, may Allaah have mercy upon him said:

---

[101] Saheeh Muslim (no. 395)

"...the Faatihah contains two means of approach, and they are: At-Tawassul by way praising, lauding, and glorification of Him and at Tawassul by way of His worship and Tawheed. Then there comes asking for the most important request and the safest desire; which is guidance, after the two means of approach. So, the supplicant, by way of it, actualizes the response.

The likes of this is the Du'aa of the Prophet ﷺ which he used to supplicate with when praying at night has been reported by Al-Bukhaaree within his Saheeh from the Hadeeth of Ibn 'Abbaas may Allaah be pleased with him that he said:

اللَّهُمَّ لَكَ الْحَمْدُ أَنْتَ نُورُ السَّمَوَاتِ وَ الْأَرْضِ وَ مَنْ فِيهِنَّ، وَ لَكَ الْحَمْدُ أَنْتَ قَيُّومُ السَّمَوَاتِ وَ الْأَرْضِ وَ مَنْ فِيهِنَّ ، وَ لَكَ الْحَمْدُ أَنْتَ الْحَقُّ، وَ وَعْدُكَ حَقٌّ ، وَ لِقَاؤُكَ حَقٌّ، وَالْجَنَّةُ حَقٌّ، وَ النَّارُ حَقٌّ، وَ النَّبِيُّونَ حَقٌّ، وَ السَّاعَةُ حَقٌّ، وَ مُحَمَّدٌ –صَلَّى اللهُ عَلَيْهِ وَسَلَّمَ –حَقٌّ، اللَّهُمَّ لَكَ أَسْلَمْتُ، وَ بِكَ آمَنْتُ ، وَ عَلَيْكَ تَوَكَّلْتُ، وَإِلَيْكَ أَنَبْتُ ، وَ بِكَ خَاصَمْتُ، وَإِلَيْكَ حَاكَمْتُ، فَاغْفِرْ لِي مَا قَدَّمْتُ وَ مَا أَخَّرْتُ، وَ مَا أَسْرَرْتُ وَ مَا أَعْلَنْتُ، أَنْتَ إِلَهِي لَا إِلَهَ إِلَّا أَنْتَ .

**'O Allaah, for you is the praise You are the
Light of the heavens and the earth and
whosoever is within them. And for You is the
praise; You are the one who sustains the
heavens and the earth and whosoever are
within them. For You is the praise; Your
Promise is the truth; meeting You is the
truth; Paradise is the truth; the Fire is the
truth; your Prophets are the truth; the Hour
is the truth; Muhammad ﷺ is the truth.
O Allaah, to You I have submitted; in You I
have believed; upon you I place my trust; to
you I turn in repentance, by way of You I
dispute; to You I refer in judgment. Forgive
me that which I have done and that which I
have not yet done; that which I have done
secretly and that which I have done openly;
You are my object of worship, none has the
right to be worshiped except You.'[102]**

*So, he mentioned At-Tawassul (seeking means of
approach) to Him by way of praising Him, lauding
Him, and worship of Him; then he asked for
forgiveness."*[103]

Al-Haafidh Ibn Hajr, may Allaah have mercy
upon him, mentioned with the explanation of
this Hadeeth:

---

[102] Saheeh (no. 1120)
[103] Madaarij As-Saalikeen 1/23-24

*"In it is the recommendation of beginning with
praise before asking, with every request; taking
him as an example."*[104]

From the examples of this is the Du'aa of Yoosuf
upon him be peace where he said:

﴿ ۞ رَبِّ قَدْ ءَاتَيْتَنِي مِنَ ٱلْمُلْكِ وَعَلَّمْتَنِي مِن تَأْوِيلِ ٱلْأَحَادِيثِ ۚ فَاطِرَ
ٱلسَّمَـٰوَٰتِ وَٱلْأَرْضِ أَنتَ وَلِـِّۦ فِي ٱلدُّنْيَا وَٱلْأَخِرَةِ ۖ تَوَفَّنِي مُسْلِمًا وَأَلْحِقْنِي
بِٱلصَّـٰلِحِينَ ﴿١٠١﴾ ﴾

**"My Lord! You have indeed bestowed on me
of the sovereignty, and taught me the
interpretation of dreams; The (only) Creator
of the heavens and the earth! You are my
Wali (Protector, Helper, Supporter, Guardian,
etc.) in this world and the Hereafter, cause
me to die as a Muslim and join me with the
righteous."[105]**

Likewise, the Du'aa of Ayyoob upon him be
peace when the most High has said:

﴿ ۞ وَأَيُّوبَ إِذْ نَادَىٰ رَبَّهُۥ أَنِّي مَسَّنِيَ ٱلضُّرُّ وَأَنتَ أَرْحَمُ ٱلرَّٰحِمِينَ ﴿٨٣﴾
فَٱسْتَجَبْنَا لَهُۥ فَكَشَفْنَا مَا بِهِۦ مِن ضُرٍّ ۖ وَءَاتَيْنَـٰهُ أَهْلَهُۥ وَمِثْلَهُم مَّعَهُمْ
رَحْمَةً مِّنْ عِندِنَا وَذِكْرَىٰ لِلْعَـٰبِدِينَ ﴿٨٤﴾ ﴾

---

[104] Fat'h Al-Baree 3/5
[105] (Yusuf 12:101)

**And (remember) Ayyoob (Job), when he cried
to his Lord: "Verily, distress has seized me,
and You are the Most Merciful of all those
who show mercy." So We answered his call,
and We removed the distress that was on
him, and We restored his family to him (that
he had lost), and the like thereof along with
them, as a mercy from Ourselves and a
Reminder for all who worship Us.**[106]

Likewise, is the supplication of those who have
an intellect; those who remember Allaah
standing, sitting, or lying upon their sides, and
who reflect on the creation of the heavens and
the earth. As Allaah mentions concerning them:

﴿رَبَّنَا مَا خَلَقْتَ هَٰذَا بَٰطِلًا سُبْحَٰنَكَ فَقِنَا عَذَابَ ٱلنَّارِ ﴿١١١﴾ ﴾

**"Our Lord! You have not created (all) this
without purpose, glory to You! Give us
salvation from the torment of the Fire."** [107]

Also, the supplication of the angels as Allaah
says:

﴿رَبَّنَا وَسِعْتَ كُلَّ شَىْءٍ رَّحْمَةً وَعِلْمًا فَٱغْفِرْ لِلَّذِينَ تَابُوا۟ وَٱتَّبَعُوا۟
سَبِيلَكَ وَقِهِمْ عَذَابَ ٱلْجَحِيمِ ﴿٧﴾ ﴾

**"Our Lord! You comprehend all things in
mercy and knowledge, so forgive those who**

---

[106] (Al-Anbiya 21:83-84)
[107] (Aali Imran 3:191)

repent and follow Your Way, and save them from the torment of the blazing Fire!" [108]

The examples of this are immensely many; to count them all would be very long. Hence, it is appropriate for the Muslim to preserve this lofty etiquette when he asks Him, Glorified be He; that he praise Him, laud Him, and Glorify Him and acknowledge His favors and blessings, then ask Him from the good of the Dunyaa and the Hereafter.

Likewise, it is appropriate for the Muslim, as well, before his Du'aa to send the prayers upon the friend and companion of Allaah, and his servant and Messenger; our Prophet Muhammad ﷺ

There has come incitement towards that within a number of Ahadeeth. From them, there is the Hadeeth of Fadaalah ibn 'Ubayd, may Allaah be pleased with him, who said:

"The Prophet heard a man supplicating within his prayer, and he did not send prayers upon the Prophet ﷺ .

So the Prophet ﷺ said:

عَجَلُ هَـذَا

'This person has been hasty.'

---

108 (Ghafir 40:7)

Then he called him and said to him and to others:

إِذَا صَلَّى أَحَدُكُمْ فَلْيَبْدَأْ بِتَحْمِيدِ اللهِ وَ الثَّنَاءِ عَلَيْهِ

ثُمَّ لِيُصَلِّ عَلَى النَّبِيِّ – صَلَّى اللهُ عَلَيْهِ وَ سَلَّمَ – ثُمَّ

لِيَدْعُ بَعْدَ بِمَا شَاءَ .

'When one of you prays then let him begin by praising Allaah and lauding Him, then let him send prayers upon the Prophet ﷺ, then let him supplicate thereafter with that which he wills.' [109]

This has three levels:

- ✓ The first is that one sends prayers upon the Prophet before the supplication, after praising Allaah.

- ✓ The second level is that one sends prayers at the beginning of the Du'aa the middle of it and the end of it.

- ✓ The third level is that one sends prayers upon him at the beginning and end, and he places that which he is in need of between the two of them.

---

[109] Reported within Al-Musnad 6/18 and Sunan Abee Daawud (no. 1481) and Sunan At-Tirmidhee (no. 3477) The 'Allaamah Al-Albaanee, may Allaah have mercy upon him, graded it Saheeh within Saheeh Al-Jaami' (no. 648)

Prayer upon the Prophet ﷺ, as it relates to Du'aa, is similar to a key. Ibnul-Qayyim, may Allaah have mercy upon him, said:

"The key to Du'aa is sending prayers upon the Prophet ﷺ just as the key to prayer is purification."

Then he transmitted from Ahmad Ibn Aboo Al-Hawraa' that he said:

"I heard Aboo Sulaymaan Ad-Daaraanee saying: 'He who wants to ask Allaah for his need then let him begin by sending prayer upon the Prophet ﷺ; then let him ask that which he needs, and let him conclude by sending prayers upon the Prophet ﷺ. For indeed, sending prayer upon the Prophet is accepted; and Allaah is too noble to reject that which is between them.'" [110]

---

[110] Jalaa' Al-Afhaam 260-262.

NOTES

NOTES

Printed in Great Britain
by Amazon